A. Drott

PSYCHOLOGY
IN THE PSALMS

A Portrait of Man in God's World

PSYCHOLOGY
IN THE PSALMS

A Portrait of Man
in God's World

Morris A. Inch

WORD BOOKS
Waco, Texas • London, England

First Printing—September 1969
Second Printing—November 1970

Preface

Not simply who but *what am I?* What is the meaning of my existence, the implications of my experience? What are my responsibilities? These and similar questions have troubled man with unrelenting persistence. He is not only interested in but gripped by the question of life.

The Christian concept of man has had a most durable history, but each generation is required to review it in the light of fresh insights from theology and the behavioral studies. To commend itself, a faith must have tangency with human experience, in order to tap its meaning, express its tragedy, and purpose its salvation. It is hoped that this work will render some service in suggesting the adequacy of the Christian faith in this regard.

Chapters 1-3 ("What is Man," "Anatomy of a Fool," and "About Face") take a new look at the nature, degradation, and salvation of man. Chapters 4 and 5 ("The Authentic Life" and "The Actualized Life") are foundation discussions of the Christian experience, suggesting the nature of the regenerate life and need of maturation. Chapters 6-9 ("Crucible of Pain," "Corporate Personality," "Meaning of Prayer," and "Martial Challenge") are treatments of critical aspects of the Christian life. Chapters 10-12 ("Retrospect," "Prospect," and "Panorama") place Christian man in time perspective, reflecting the meaning of history, hope, and present help.

Selected psalms are employed as the basis of this study. The text is a free translation and the commentary assumes their nature as Christian literature. The approach taken is experiential. The question asked of the Biblical text is: "What does it mean for me?" The answer comes not only by way of Scripture but through extra-Biblical materials, in order to clarify, express and apply the principles derived. The result is, in the best sense of the word, an apologetic. It is a rationale for faith in the twentieth century.

No verse-by-verse exegesis of the text should be expected.

Instead, the psalm is first viewed in its totality as a guide to some perplexing facet of experience. A more detailed investigation follows, searching out something of the psalm's abiding message for contemporary man. The measure of success will be determined by the commentary's ability to apply the eternal message, albeit imperfectly, to life as we experience it.

Acknowledgements

This book is about life, the lessons for which I am indebted to countless persons, among whom were considerate parents, enjoyable sisters and brother, and faithful friends. The effort to focus in on life is a task in which I have been aided by the critical advice of Martha Hook on a trial chapter, Doctors Millard Ericksen, Harold Lindsell, and Samuel Shultz on the rough draft, typing assistance from Bertha Caine and Dorothy Rung, and especially the personal encouragement of my beloved wife Joan.

Contents

— 1 —
What Is Man?

p 11

To know God as He is is to begin to understand one's self. Otherwise man walks the peculiar twilight zone between beast and God. He is repulsed by the jungle code but sits uneasily on the throne of self-worship.

What Is Man?

*To the choir director, according to Gittith.
A psalm of David.*

1. Yahweh* our Lord, how glorious is Your name in all the earth; who appoints Your majesty over the heavens.
2. With the mouth of children and infants You have decreed strength because of Your enemies, to still the enemy and the avenger.
3. When I view Your heavens, the work of Your fingers, the moon and the stars, which You have established;
4. What is mortal man that You should consider him, and the son of man, that You should take oversight of him?
5. Yet You have made him little less than divinity, and have crowned him with glory and majesty.
6. You have given him rule over the works of Your hands; You have laid all things under his feet,
7. All sheep and oxen, and also the beasts of the field,
8. The birds of the air, and the fish of the sea, (whatever) passes in the mode of the seas.
9. Yahweh, our Lord, how glorious is Your name in all the earth.

PSALM 8

---

* The name Yahweh is an approximate rendering of the Hebrew name for God which is translated LORD in the King James Version and Jehovah in the American Standard Version.

The most pressing and persistent question for man concerns the nature of his existence. The question cries aloud for attention and pleads for resolution.

MAN UNDERSTOOD IN RELATION TO GOD

The psalmist begins his quest for life's meaning with God (vs. 4). He accepts the testimony that man is created in the image of the Almighty (cf. Gen. 1:26). He implies that the knowledge of God is the first step toward self-discovery.

To know God as He is is to begin to understand one's self. Otherwise, man walks the peculiar twilight zone between beast and God. He is repulsed by the jungle code but sits uneasily on the throne of self-worship. While his conscience is disturbed by a visit to the harlot's house he is awed in the great cathedral.

His Name Is "Yahweh"

Who is the One of whom man is said to be the image? He is called Yahweh, a term most likely derived from the idea of being (vs. 1). The ancient world was populated with gods; there was a general agreement to tolerate all gods, while courting the favor of certain local deities. Yahweh was revealed to the Hebrews as the only true God, the Living One, the I Am. The opening words of the Decalogue read: "I am Yahweh your God, who brought you out of the land of Egypt, out of the house of bondage. You shall have no other gods before me" (Exod. 20:2-3).* Yahweh prohibited belief in and worship of the pantheon. The pleas of Joshua uncompromisingly echoed the first commandment: "Choose you this day whom you will serve; whether the gods which your fathers served that were on the other side of the flood or the gods of the Amorites, in whose land you dwell; but as for me and my house, we will serve Yahweh" (Josh. 24:15).

As for man, his life is fleeting. "His days are as grass: as a flower of the field; so he flourishes, for the wind passes over it, and

---

* All Scripture quotations, unless otherwise noted, are drawn or modified from the King James Version.

it is gone" (Psa. 103:15-16a). Man's life is derived from and dependent upon God, for only Yahweh is self-existent. Only He in this sense is.

Let Him Be God

Although man's knowledge of God may be accurate, it is never exhaustive; so the earth declares His name but cannot contain it (vs. 1). Man is limited to creation in his investigation (vss. 6-8). He employs the microscope and the telescope, discriminates and correlates, and stores the results of his experimentation in great libraries. Nothing in God's creation is safely hidden from him except, in a qualified sense, himself (vs. 4).

Idolatry is the failure to let God be God. In idolatry man contradicts the divine nature and in so doing distorts his own. His person can no longer reflect the One with whom he fails to reckon.

Divine-Human Relationship

God is not only transcendent but personal (vs. 4). He who framed the world communes with people. As a result, man may not only know about God but may actually know Him.

This is not to say that God can be approached as equal, for this would violate reality and abort the valued relationship (vss. 1, 9). Idolatry assumes a relationship between man and God but rejects the necessary conditions. It offers, but does not exercise, obedience to Yahweh. Communion is completely lacking.

Coupled with obedience to God's way is responsibility to His world (vss. 5-8). From the first pruning of Eden's foliage to the last orbit of earth's surface, man's stewardship will be required of him. Viktor Frankl says: "Ultimately, man should not ask what the meaning of his life is but rather he must recognize that it is he who is asked. In a word, each man is questioned by life; and he can only answer to life by answering for his own life; to life he can only respond by being responsible."[1] Frankl does not mean

[1]Viktor Frankl, *Man's Search For Meaning*, p. 11. This and subsequent

to discredit man's quest for self-meaning, but to suggest that it can only be found in answering the question of responsibility.

Obligation is the "given" of human existence. To be human is to be obligated. We may not know how and to whom we are accountable, but we cannot doubt that we are responsible creatures.

After the Korean conflict, a G.I. was questioned about his behavior in prison camp. He and several other prisoners had dragged a man suffering from dysentery out of the barracks and had left him in the snow to freeze to death. When confronted with the report, the soldier protested: "You can't blame me for doing that. I wasn't responsible." But no amount of contradiction excuses him from liability. The court was free to weigh extenuating circumstances, but not to dismiss the charge. (Responsibility) is the nature of life, the datum of human experience.

The psalmist does not have to tell us of our obligation, but he does tell us to whom we are accountable, and he outlines the nature of our responsibility. Yahweh is Lord. His moral law is the description of duty, and His will is the extension of it.

We might suppose that a relationship of obedience and responsibility with God would be grievous. The psalmist's experience was quite the opposite (vss. 1-2, 9). Jesus promised: "Take my yoke upon you, and learn from me; for I am gentle and lowly in heart, and you will find rest for your souls. For my yoke is easy, and my burden is light" (Matt. 11:29-30, RSV). God is not perverse in His judgment nor arbitrary in His demands. He is exacting in love and gentle in correction.

The world's taskmasters ask much and give little in return, but Yahweh supplies grace commensurate with man's duties. The note of sufficiency is implicit at the outset of the psalm, and explicit in verse 4. The idea is beautifully reflected elsewhere: "Whom have I in heaven but You? There is none upon earth that I desire beside You. My flesh and my heart fail, but God is the strength of my heart, and my portion for ever" (Psa. 73:25-26). God is no man's debtor. The prodigal finds no sustenance in a far country, but abundance in the Father's house.

Man in Perspective

"The poet regards man in the light of the purpose for which he was created."[2] The picture is of man as he was ideally conceived, a necessary reminder for each generation. Contemporary studies of man measure his affinity to brute beast, and trace his origin from the organic elements. We run a reluctant rat through the maze to help us better understand ourselves. We conduct threshold-of-life experiments to bridge the gap between the living and the nonliving. Man, however, was formed not only of the dust of the ground but by the breath of God. He needs to look up to gain perspective and discover that he is in the image of the Most High.

The point is not to discredit laboratory research or to minimize the difficulty of investigating the human being. E. C. Tolman concludes: "Personally . . . I am suspicious of . . . verbal reports. I prefer to try to work out psychology with the aid of more gross forms of behavior. My motto for the present is: 'Rats, up men.'"[3] Earlier, Tolman dedicated one of his works to the white rat with which he had experimented. However, there are dangers to this approach which Frankl describes as "the teaching of man's nothingbutness." While appreciating the dilemma of self-analysis, we must beware of the approach which reduces man to less than the person who asks: "Who am I?"

Scripture teaches us that man is a person, a human being as opposed to a thing or an animal (vss. 6-8). He not only experiences but reflects upon his existence. He is self-conscious and capable of raising the question of meaning (vs. 4). The most important factor in his quest for understanding is that he is created in the image of God (vs. 5). Man is not the measure of God, but God is the measure of man. For all our knowledge *about* man, God is the source of our knowledge *of* him.

God transcends man but reveals Himself to him (vss. 1, 9). Therefore man may not only know *about* God, but may actually know Him in a personal way. But he cannot know God as an

---

[2]Franz Delitzsch, *Biblical Commentary on the Psalms*, I, 156.
[3]Stephen Strasser, *Phenomenology and the Human Sciences*, p. 12.

equal, for Yahweh is revealed as Lord. Man finds God only as he searches with all his being (Deut. 4:29), and acknowledges the divine claim on his life (Deut. 4:31). Far from finding this a grievous situation (vss. 1, 9), man discovers his highest fulfillment in relationship to the Almighty (vs. 5).

Man Out of Focus

The psalmist also shows us that man is no longer in perspective. Man has rejected God and therefore may be described as the enemy and the avenger (vs. 2). He assumes the role of enemy, when he turns against the Creator. He takes the avenger's right in that he rejects God's justice and despises His prerogatives. Jesus applied this verse in a similar fashion, shaming the impervious religious leaders with the warm response of the populace (Matt. 21:16).

The author of Hebrews quoted extensively from this psalm, when he was showing man's "transgression and disobedience" (Heb. 2:2) and failure to achieve his noble ideal (Heb. 2:8). Jesus is the true man who is obedient to God and restores man to fellowship with Him (Heb. 2:9-11). Unfortunately man is reluctant to admit his defection or accept God's grace. As Carl Jung observes, man has "the determination to maintain the present synthesis at all costs."[4]

Man's difficulty is not simply ignorance of his nature, but wilful disobedience of God. We shall want to consider the nature of this defection and its resolution at length in later chapters, but it will suffice for now to point out that man as he experiences himself is fallen from the relationship which gives meaning to self. He needs not only reorientation but repentance. The only road is the road back.

MAN'S VIEW OF HIMSELF

Man has made extensive and numerous efforts to determine the meaning of his existence. In this section, however, we shall limit ourselves to a brief commentary on the three schools of Viennese

---

[4]David Cox, *Jung and St. Paul*, p. 45.

psychotherapy, and the way in which these seem to compare with the Biblical norm. In so doing, we must take care not to identify Biblical language too closely with psychological counterparts. Our interpretation of both the revealed Word and human experience is less than absolute.

Sigmund Freud

Freud supposed that the key to man's existence is the will to pleasure. Whatever disposes of a need satisfies. Man consists of id, ego, and superego. The id is the primitive animal nature of man, located in the unconscious. It constantly strives to gratify the libido, the energy by which needs are directed. The superego is an internalization of the limitations placed upon the quest for pleasure. The ego is man's rational self, which controls the id urges and represses them into the unconscious. "According to Freud the ego strives to establish balance among the three 'tyrants' —id, superego, and outer environment."[5] His view may be called homeostatic; i.e., it explains man's existence as an effort to maintain a pleasant adaptation of life.

That man has needs, ranging from metabolic—such as oxygen, food, water, and elimination—to those of personal integration—such as love and a sense of worth—is quite certain. But it is not so certain whether the quest for need-satisfaction is a sufficient explanation for the human dynamic. What of the destructive forces in man? What of the adaptation of forces in terms of goals? What of voluntary acceptance of tension? What of the ideals around which life is organized?

Alfred Adler

The deficiency in Freud's view of man can be seen in part in the rebellion of his brilliant student Adler. While Freud had given primacy to the libido—that energy by which the id forces are released—Adler emphasized the ego—the effort of man to at-

---

[5]Gordon W. Allport, "The Open System in Personality Theory," *Theories of Personality*, Lindzey and Hall, eds., p. 234.

tain superiority. Adler believed that man suffers from a psychic inferiority, an inferiority complex. The dynamic of man's existence is the will to power.

The psalmist exhibits this characteristic. He is overwhelmed by the expanse and permanence of the universe and feels small and fragile by comparison. He further shares with Adler the conviction that man is not simply at the mercy of unconscious forces, but regulates these in terms of goals. Compensation may be a factor, as is the gratification of needs. But from the poet's point of view there is an obvious lack in this picture of man. The note of responsibility is missing. What of man's sense of *ought*, the moral rectitude which plays so large a role in his decision-making?

Viktor Frankl

We have characterized Freud's view as the will to pleasure, and Adler's interpretation as the will to power. Viktor Frankl's alternative is the will to meaning. "Values . . . do not drive a man; they do not *push* him, but rather *pull* him."[6] Frankl thinks that meaning is not invented by man but rather detected. It is found in decision based upon responsible action.

Frankl reflects the Hebraic feeling for man's accountability. Man is not simply generic—a museum variety—but actualized—an individual living responsibly. Frankl, however, seems to have discarded the companion element in his heritage, the prophetic nature of man's existence. God speaks to man through His servants, defining the source and nature of responsibility. Otherwise, every man does that which is right in his own sight (Judg. 21:25). Revelation is not immediate—that is, perceived by every sincere man in his moment of decision. Rather it is mediate—made available and mediated by the prophetic word.

Man's life is marked off, separated, from both God and beast. His eyes sweep the heavens. Behind the work he senses a power. Behind the artistic order he perceives an architect. Man is capable of religious meditation, and he is probably unique in this regard. My cat likes the moonlit nights, but I doubt if he sees

---

[6]Frankl, *op. cit.*, p. 101.

anything of God's writing in the sky. Man, being himself capable of complex symbolism and script, can appreciate the large hand of God across the heavens.

Man also surveys the brute world about him, which he super-intends in a godlike role. Man is not one of the brutes, although there is an affinity. He is not God either, although there is a similarity. A human being is a peculiar entity, a responsible creature, finding in the application of revelation to decision-making his individual purpose in life. This is the nature of his existence. Man is responsible to God and liable for God's creation. Gratification is found in purpose, fulfillment in the responsible life.

ELABORATION OF MAN'S NATURE

The fundamental thing about man is his unity. "The Hebrew idea of personality is that of an animated body, not (like the Greek) that of an incarnated soul."[7] He "as a unity could have a hundred different aspects and a hundred different words to describe them. . . . The one fact that remained clear was that man, with all his diversity of aspects, was an integral unity."[8]

Biblical man is a sensate being. The two most common words used to express this fact are flesh (basar, sarx), and body (soma). "Each stands for the whole man differently regarded, man as wholly perishable (sarx), man as wholly designated for God (soma)."[9] The body is not evil per se. It is perhaps the idea that body binds man to the world order, which is antagonistic to God, that gives rise to certain moral distinctions.

Here is a watershed in the conception of human existence. Oriental religious thought has tended to treat existence as an illu-sion, a misconception of the nature of reality. On this premise the solution to man's dilemma is to snuff out all that reminds him that he is. The psalmist makes the realistic assumption: the world has objective reality. Man too is earthy—he perspires, aches, senses pleasure. The key to life is found in the fact that he was made

---

[7]Wheeler Robinson, The Christian Doctrine of Man, p. 27.
[8]W. David Stacy, The Pauline View of Man, p. 223.
[9]Stacy, op. cit., p. 184.

for God's glory, to commune with his Creator. His aspirations are real, as are his frustrations. He accepts life as the gift of God.

Man is a rational being. He thinks. Man can review the past, analyze the present, and prepare for the future. Some of the more common terms used by the Biblical writers to express this purpose are soul (nephesh, psyche), spirit (ruach, pneuma), mind (nous, dianois), heart (leb, lebah, libbah, kardia), and kidney (kelayoth, nephros). "Soul" and "spirit" are used at times interchangeably. When a distinction is intended, it seems to be to stress the relationship of mind to body (soul), and mind to God and spiritual qualities (spirit). Nous refers to mind in its distinctively intellectual aspects. While "heart" and "kidney" can also be used to express the rational aspect of man, it is not clear whether or not any peculiar meaning is intended by their substitution for the other available terms.

The psalmist is clearly a rational man. He considers the meaning of the heavens, surveys the adversaries and the youthful ranks of the defenders, reflects on the feebleness and nobility of man, and magnifies the name of God. He makes the rationalistic assumption: man is capable of thought activity.

Man is an emotional creature. Emotion, a compound of e (out of) and movere (to move), suggests being moved out of rest. Leander Keyser classifies emotions as: (1) sentient—corresponding to sense perception; (2) intuitional—immediate perception of reality, and (3) psychical—connected with understanding.[10] Man feels positively, negatively, or ambivalently toward a given stimulus, and the intensity of his emotion varies. "Heart" and "kidney" are the more likely terms used by Biblical writers to express this aspect of man. "Heart" may be used not only to distinguish feeling from intellect, but to portray the wholeness of man's response in contrast to an intellectual accent. "From the heart springs conduct; both good and bad. Emotions, decisions, intentions or judgment, seated in the heart, may be praiseworthy or otherwise."[11] "Kidney" refers to the innermost aspect of man, but its peculiar distinctive (if such exists) is uncertain.

[10]Leander Keyser, A Handbook of Christian Psychology, pp. 128-131.
[11]Stacy, op. cit., p. 196.

The emotions of the psalmist are vividly expressed. There are the threshold feelings of the night—the coolness against his flesh, the soft whisper of air after a drying day, the earth oozing between his toes, the sound of a distant dog protesting an intrusion, the sparkle of light against the pitch-black sky.

There were the intuitive feelings of the soul—the sense of unworthiness, the awareness of danger, the presence of God, the joy of being. There were the feelings accompanying understanding—the glory of the God who has revealed Himself, the safety of the people for whom God does battle, the perfection of God's purpose and plan for man. These and more the psalmist felt.

Man is a volitional creature. He is not simply acted upon, the product of external forces, but he acts, creating history and culture. "Will" (ratson, thelema) is the term which conveys this meaning. The will is not of or in itself bad; but when it is set against the will of God it is both wrong and in need of control by man's rational nature. Man can respond, and is held accountable for his action. Late in the history of Israel it became customary to blame adverse circumstances on the sins of the fathers. It was said: "The fathers have eaten sour grapes, and the children's teeth are set on edge." Ezekiel disallowed the proverb: "The soul that sins shall die. But if a man is just . . . he shall surely live, says the Lord God" (Ezek. 18:4-5, 9b). The poet sees the array of God's self-determined adversaries, and counts himself among those who choose the camp of Yahweh.

When Yahweh spoke to Moses out of the flaming bush, He introduced Himself as "the God of Abraham, the God of Isaac, and the God of Jacob" (Exod. 3:15). These were flesh-and-blood, historical people, the ancestors of Moses. They were men who thought, felt, and willed. Above all, they were men of faith. They realized the spiritual dimension of life, that they were made in God's image and for His purpose. To realize this truth is to raise "mankind to a level in the universe where decisive things happen in every moment, decisive for the ultimate meaning of all existence. In each of us such decisions occur, in us, and through us. This is our burden. This is our despair. This is our greatness."[12]

---

[12]Paul Tillich, The Eternal Now, p. 57.

The lowliness of man's origin is seen in his title son of Adam—he was created from the dust. The greatness of man can be recognized in what God made him—but a little lower than divinity. "The word 'elohim' is capable of . . . three interpretations, since it means either a divine being (god), or divine beings (angels) or the divine being par excellence (God). The context must be our guide to its sense."[13] Man was created but a little lower than the supernatural beings. He is both at home, and yet in a foreign land. His is a pilgrimage toward a life for which he was intended and even now realizes in part.

We should "emphasize the fact that it is *God who has crowned him with glory and honor,* so that any self-crowning is, like boasting, 'excluded;' and to point out further that all man does in relation to nature is to find out God's secrets, not to invent them."[14] Human experience is prone to extremes. It exalts itself unduly and despairs in the face of frustration. The text has a very practical application. When battered by life's circumstances, man may take comfort in the continued attention of God, and find in such moments the solace and strength of the Almighty. When impressed by his *own* attainments, man needs to reflect on his frailty, with appropriate thankfulness to God for His sustaining grace. Man's exalted place is the result of grace, God's unmerited favor.

God commanded man to subdue the earth and have dominion over it (Gen. 1:28). Man, under God, is ordained to reign over the created universe. Perhaps this idea can best be expressed by saying that man's responsibility is to subdue all things *unto God.* The logical components of this mandate are knowledge, relationship, and authority. Man must investigate his domain to determine its composition and detail. He relates life to God, avoiding the arbitrary distinction between secular and sacred. He exercises control over nature, subjecting it to worthwhile ends.

There follows in verses 7 and 8 of the psalm what is apparently a reference to the general categories of animal life. There are the domesticated animals small and large, the undomesticated animals of the field, the inhabitants of the air, the fish of the sea, and such

[13]William R. Taylor, *The Interpreter's Bible,* IV, p. 52.
[14]J. R. P. Sclater, *Ibid.*

other creatures which dwell in the waters. Man's rule over the natural order is complete. He has the power to domesticate, and can destroy. Nothing of the natural order challenges his reign.

The psalmist uses what were to him the most obvious illustrations of man's supremacy. Another author in a later day might have pointed to medical research or space travel as evidence of man's control. Conquest of the animal world is generally taken for granted today, but man's prowess continues to be expressed in a myriad of ways. Creation is his charge, life his opportunity, and God's grace his salvation.

CONTEMPORARY MAN'S DILEMMA

The subject of man has been developed at some length, following the guide of the psalmist's perspective, stopping by the three schools of Viennese psychotherapy, and traveling along the path of Biblical explication. While the Scriptural idea of man may be better in focus, we cannot assume that twentieth-century man's dilemma in this regard is understood. It remains to suggest the nature of his difficulty.

Julian Hartt says of contemporary man:

> We are having great difficulty in getting a clear, steady, and amiable image of ourselves. Lacking this center of reference (Hebrew-Christian) for understanding and evaluation, we are strongly inclined to accept whatever dogma and image is doing a brisk business in the market, even if they are incompatible either with the good conscience of conventionality or the demands of creativity.[15]

Still, the Christian doctrine of man "has so passed into the common stock of our higher Western thought as to be the chief formative influence in our conception of personality. Our familiarity with our unconscious dependence upon it may result in the failure to do justice to it."[16] Western man still senses something of the psalmist's idea of man, but he is having increasing difficulty

---

[15]Julian N. Hartt, *The Lost Image of Man*, p. 6.
[16]Robinson, *op. cit.*, p. 3.

getting the image into focus. There is a feeling of unreality about it all. Life seems meaningless and empty, not simply vacuous, but emptied of Christian meaning. The shell remains, but the content is lacking. T. S. Eliot's confession of the hollow men is doubtless the honest expression of many:

> We are the hollow men
> We are the stuffed men
> Leaning together
> Headpiece filled with straw. Alas!
> Our dried voices, when
> We whisper together
> Are quiet and meaningless
> As wind in dry grass
> Or rats' feet over broken glass
> In our dry cellar.[17]

Such is contemporary man's predicament; the Biblical image haunts his despair. The confident refrain of the psalmist is in the sharpest contrast to his perplexity: "Yahweh, our Lord, how glorious is Your name in all the earth" (vs. 7).

The issue, in Paul Tillich's words, is a matter of "ultimate concern." Man's self-image is the measure of his potential. Its degeneracy is invitation to disaster. Conceived as a machine, man may strive for economic proficiency, but he lacks personal values. As a beast, he may gratify biological needs but falls short of humanistic ideals. His code will reflect to a startling degree his self-appraisal. He is capable of a predatory life, imitating the jungle law of survival.

A still greater danger is that man will think himself a god. The beast preys to satisfy hunger, but the god assumes life and death prerogative over his fellows regardless of personal need. As a god, man usurps the due process of law in deference to his supposed omniscience, and in doing so may feel little responsibility for his action or reverence for the personality of another. No threat to

---

[17]T. S. Eliot, "The Hollow Men," *Collected Poems 1909-1962*. Copyright, 1936, by Harcourt, Brace & World, Inc.; copyright © 1963, 1964 by T. S. Eliot. Reprinted by permission of the publisher.

man's survival compares with the unloosing of a caste of gods, a superrace.

The psalmist's image of man commends itself, not simply because of its potential for keeping man in check, but because of its correlation to human experience. The question is not what we would profit from being, but what man is. By way of example, in a recent interview a Russian college youth confessed that he failed to live up to the golden rule: "Do to others as you would have them do unto you." In other words, the image of man provided by economic materialism was not sufficient for this young man; it failed to account for his experience of moral rectitude and moral disparity. He was unwittingly modifying the party line to accommodate for the meaning of existence. But having taken a step toward self-understanding, he was barred from the divine point of reference, which would have illuminated his nature.

The persisting problem was shockingly illustrated for many Americans by the murder of Kitty Genovese, a young woman whose pleas for help were ignored by scores of persons in an apartment building facing the scene of her struggle for life. The reason for the failure has been variously interpreted, but the problem seems to lie deeper than the fear of involvement. It reflects an anonymity, an inability to grasp self-meaning and the responsibility which is related to it.

SUMMARY

There are many facets to man's experience, but at the heart is his search for meaning, his abiding sense of liability. The world is the scene of but not the solution to his quest. "For the self which stands outside of itself and the world cannot find the meaning of life in itself or the world. It cannot identify meaning with causality in nature; for its freedom is obviously something different from the causal links of nature."[18] The Scripture provides man with the explanation that he is responsible to God in terms of the application of His moral law.

Man is further described in connection with his sensate nature,

---

[18]Reinhold Niebuhr, *The Nature and Destiny of Man*, I, p. 14.

and his rational, emotional, and volitional capacities. He is brought sharply into focus for contemporary man, struggling as he is for self-identity.

God is needed in order to understand existential man. Reject Him and man loses perspective: "Because that, when they knew God, they glorified him not as God, neither were thankful; but became vain in their imaginations, and their foolish heart was darkened" (Rom. 1:21). Dissolution is assured. But exalt Yahweh and man is ennobled; he becomes the servant of the Most High—the creature whose destiny is linked with the Eternal. Life then is no longer an idle pretense, but a glorious drama of divine-human relationship.

2

Anatomy of a Fool

The fool will not recognize God, but he cannot escape Him. Through historical events, by the witness of the redeemed, the Almighty awakens man to the reality which he tries desperately to repress—that God is present. The Hound of Heaven allows man no hiding place. Man's anxiety results, then, not merely from his finiteness but from the fact that he is a frustrated fugitive.

le nol how 'arrival (Ching) become ne—
long ... men revert to arrival. Actual
is heart — In arrival below
butte.
They do it lead to
each other..

Anatomy of a Fool

To the choir director of David.

1. The fool says in his heart, There is no God. They are corrupt. They perform abhorrent practices. There is none that does good.
2. Yahweh looked over from the heavens upon the sons of men, to see if there were any to understand, that seek God.
3. They all have turned aside. They are alike contaminated. There is none which does good, truly, not one.
4. Have the workers of iniquity no knowledge, who devour my people as they eat bread, and do not call upon Yahweh?
5. There they tremble in fear, for God is with the generation of the righteous.
6. You would discredit the deliberation of the humble, because the Lord is his refuge.
7. Who will give deliverance of Israel out of Zion? When Yahweh returns his people from captivity, Jacob shall rejoice, and Israel shall be glad.

PSALM 14

*Proper diagnosis is normally a necessary step toward
remedy. Having seen evidence of man's disorder and located
the difficulty in the general area of his defection from God,
we need to identify the problem more specifically. Otherwise,
we may mistake the symptom for the cause, the analgesic for
the cure.*

FOLLY OF DISBELIEF

The fool asserts that there is no God (vs. 1). No exception is
made to the rule. *Nabal* (fool) suggests being withered, lacking
vitality. It does not imply a general deficiency of knowledge or
of mental acumen, but a lack of comprehension and realization of
life's meaning.

Man is to be understood in relation to God. The relationship
implies moral rectitude on man's part, as one Rabbinic commentary suggests: "But where do we find [warnings against] the
opinions of the heretics, and the hankering after immorality and
idolatry? It has been taught: 'After your own heart.' This refers
to heresy, and so it says: 'The fool hath said in his heart, there is
no God.' "[1] Man's defection is at once from God *and* the good
life.

How well have our contemporaries fathomed the dual aspect
of man's default? Erich Fromm distinguishes between authori-
tarian religion, as belief that a man is controlled by a power outside himself, and humanistic religion, as faith in the expression
of man's own potential.[2] The result is a false dichotomy, where
man must choose between God and the good life. He cannot
develop his own potential without breaking away from divine
shackles.

Paul Tillich's view is at this point more amenable to the text of
the psalm. He continually uses the terms heteronomy, autonomy,
and theonomy. "Heteronomy" refers to the imposition of law
upon man from outside, "autonomy" to the rule of self, and

---

[1] *Berakoth*, 12b. *The Babylonian Talmud*.
[2] Erich Fromm, *Psychoanalysis and Religion*, pp. 34-64.

"theonomy" to the existence of a superior law rooted in God and in harmony with man's true nature. A wrong normally presupposes a right relationship to existing conditions. An analogy, while less than exact, may help clarify the point. The child is scolded for tracking in mud on his mother's clean floor. But it is all right for him to track mud around as he scampers around the yard. What is the difference? The situation, the purpose, and the persons involved make the difference. This is not to say that the rule of wiping one's feet is arbitrary; the mother knows that cleanliness in the living quarters is a most desirable goal. A failure to uphold her rule would be harmful and wrong, not simply or primarily in connection with the floor, but out of concern for the welfare of the youngster.

In similar fashion, theonomy expresses the idea that life has a moral purposefulness. God does not shift the rules of existence to accommodate an individual's preference. His rigorous and relentless justice firms up man's moral integrity and health.

A CLINICAL DECAGON

The poet-analyst proceeds to describe man's dilemma from ten vantage points. He piles up observations as if to establish beyond any shadow of doubt the true and critical nature of the difficulty.

First observation: the fool is corrupt (vs. 1). The term *shachath* is used in Jeremiah 13:7 of the decomposition of a buried waistcloth, and in Leviticus 22:25 of a blemished offering. Serviceability is the key thought. The psalmist sees man as thoroughly useless to the Creator.

Second observation: he performs abhorrent practices (vs. 1). The Hebrew word *taab* implies an intense, even painful physical repulsion. The Latin roots of "abhor" *(ab*—from; *horrēre*—stiffen with horror), suggest the depth of the aversion. The idea is particularly appropriate where the offender is seen to violate the prescribed reverence and worship of God. Antiochus Epiphanes' sacrifice of the swine on the temple altar, and the required Jewish participation in the orgy associated with the worship of Bacchus are good examples. The psalmist reckons that man's offense amounts to profanation and open impiety.

Third observation: he does no good (vss. 1, 3). The richness of the Hebrew word *tab* can be seen in the associated ideas of piety, gladness, benevolence, and pleasure (Psa. 37:27; Gen. 1:4). It expresses the wholesome state, one which the viewer describes as thoroughly lacking in man.

Fourth observation: he does not understand (vs. 2). The psalmist uses a word *(sakal)* which means to see life in true perspective. It is to live righteously—consistent with the will of God; artfully—sensitive to the needs of others; and enthusiastically—expressive of the fulfilled life. The psalmist sees man as falling utterly short of the ideal.

Fifth observation: he does not seek God (vs. 2). The word "seek" *(darash)* was used of inquiring at an oracle, as for guidance in a military enterprise. Unfortunately, the pagan oracles tended to be very ambiguous. When King Croesus attempted to discover the success of his proposed venture against Cyrus, the oracle reported that a great kingdom would fall as a result of his campaign. Croesus failed to ask which empire, and so committed his armies and his empire to defeat. The psalmist assumes no such ambiguity with Yahweh, but notes that man seeks no counsel whatever.

Sixth observation: he turns aside (sur) (vs. 3). To turn aside *(sur)* implies not merely a wrong turn, but the turning of one's back (Jer. 2:21). This amounts to apostasy and degeneracy of life. Man's back is turned, and his steps lead him away from high ground.

Seventh observation: he is contaminated (vs. 3). Of all the descriptions, this one is most accessible to the senses. The word for contaminated *(alab)* calls to mind the souring of milk or the putrid odor of rotten meat. It is as if the writer wished to describe the decomposition of man before his eyes, and the nauseous stench that fills the air.

Eighth observation: he works vanity (vs. 4). "Vanity" *(owen)* suggests emptiness, falsehood, and wickedness. Man has turned life upside down. He lives in a topsy-turvy and illusory world of his own creation.

Ninth observation: he devours God's people (vs. 4). The circumstances which gave rise to the indictment are not known. The context seems to suggest military conflict, and perhaps the abandonment and relish with which evil men slaughter and spoil. The inhumanity of man for man, and more particularly of evil men for those who enjoy a covenant with Yahweh, draws a gasp of disbelief from the psalmist.

Tenth observation: he does not call on Yahweh (vs. 4). What is implied by this judgment is not certain. It may suggest an appeal for help, a summons, or the praise of God. The last of these alternatives is especially tempting; thanklessness is the first step away from God (Rom. 1:21). Man turns his heart in thanklessness, before his back in apathy, or his hand to hostility. No encouraging word of praise is heard upon the fool's lips.

The psalmist has gone to considerable length to describe the extent of man's depravity. The fool has perverted life's meaning: he has distintegrated the moral nature of his being, directed evil toward others, and turned against the Sustainer of life.

DIAGNOSIS

"In Adam all die" (I Cor. 15:22a). Man has fallen from the state which provided him with life and health. The psalmist's clinical observation reflects the extent of his lapse.

Complex Personal Evil

Human depravity expresses itself in an imaginative variety. It is sometimes gross, more often subtle, but always complex. There is, however, a common denominator. It is this factor for which we search in turning to the Genesis account.

Adam was placed in an orchard which bore plentifully and with variety (Gen. 2:9). Cultivation of the trees was to be his task, and the produce used to sustain his life (Gen. 2:15-16). The fruit of one tree was prohibited, that of the tree of knowledge of good and evil (Gen. 2:17). "The antonyms 'good and evil' mean 'everything' here. (See also Genesis 24:50, Zephaniah 1:12 and Proverbs 15:3). The same expression in inverted order occurs in Egyptian, where 'evil-good' means 'everything'."[3] The accent is on "good and evil" instead of "knowledge."

[3] Cyrus H. Gordon, *The World of the Old Testament*, p. 36.

It is man's effort to alter all of life around himself, rather than a depreciation of knowledge, that constitutes his problem.[4] As a creature whose principle of existence lies in Another, he has tried to set up his life on its own, and to exist for himself. Man's defection involves not only alienation—the rending of fellowship—but degradation—the breaking of moral law. Adam rationalized his course of action (Gen. 3:6), but found it to result in alienation from God (Gen. 3:23), and perversion of His holy will for man (Gen. 3:3, 17-19). Adam had violated theonomous law.

John Milton captures human presumption in these words of Adam who is wondering whether or not to eat the forbidden fruit with Eve:

> . . . inducement strong
> To us, as likely tasting to attain
> Proportional ascent, which cannot be
> But to be Gods, or Angel Demi-gods.
> Nor can I think that God, Creator wise,
> Though threatening, will in earnest so destroy
> Us his prime Creatures, dignifi'd so high . . .[5]

So man thought that God's law was arbitrarily conceived, or could be readily bent to accommodate his perversion. God is more, but certainly not less, than the moral ground of man's being. Man's sin may be variously viewed and described, but its derivation is always the same: theonomous law has been defied.

Compound Social Evil

Scripture tells of an angel with flaming sword guarding the entrance to Eden. Within is the tree of life; without are Adam and his progeny. Paul quotes Psalm 14 at length in this connection (Rom. 3:10-12). No man has access—all have sinned. Both "Jews and Greeks are all under sin" (Rom. 3:9), and "all have sinned and fall short of the glory of God" (Rom. 3:23). Paul did not use

---

[4] For alternative interpretations of the meaning of "good and evil" see Marcus Dodds, *Genesis*, p. 11, and F. S. C. Northrup, *Man, Nature, and God*, p. 44.

[5] John Milton, *Paradise Lost*, IX, 934-940.

the psalm as a proof text as such, but as an indication of the fact for which he argues. His thesis is developed in connection with the obligation to preach to both Jew and Greek (Rom. 1:16). It is grounded in the natural revelation of God (Rom. 1:20), and is reflected in the rebellion of the pagan (Rom. 1:21-32) and Jew (Rom. 2:1f). Sin has reigned since Adam (Rom. 5:14). Paul stresses the universality of the fault; David stresses the thoroughness of man's depravity.

The effects of human solidarity can hardly be exaggerated. The individual is one *of* and *with* mankind. The results of personal choice reenter as control, not only in the individual life, but as social heritage. So pervasive is the effect, that modern psychology and sociology are patently deterministic in outlook, allowing little or no place for human freedom. The belief that time will somehow eradicate sin is hopelessly naïve. Defection and rebellion are only intensified by a process of devolution (Rom. 1:21-32).

The process of human corruption is accelerated by the adversary, Satan. This antithetical spirit is called the god of this world (II Cor. 4:4), and an angel of light who sends forth his servants as apostles of truth (II Cor. 11:13-15). His subtle contrivance stops short of no device, employing even those persons and institutions overtly dedicated to God's service. Man is enticed and coerced in his rebellion against theonomous law.

Anxiety

The result of human defection is anxiety (cf. Gen. 3:8), suggesting a mental torment caused by a state of uncertainty. While fear implies a rather well-defined object, "anxiety, on the other hand, is a vague, pervasive experience. It enshrouds its victims, moves along with them, makes escape virtually impossible."[6] Soren Kierkegaard seems to say that anxiety is the precondition to sin—the realization of free choice. While this is in a sense true, I prefer to think of anxiety as the result of sin, coming from the abuse of freedom. The dread of which we speak should not be confused with concern over an impending danger which is

---

[6]Robert Woodworth, *Contemporary Schools of Psychology*, p. 320.

normal anxiety, or with an unrealistic foreboding—abnormal anxiety. This dread is rather part of the nature of fallen life itself —existential anxiety.

Death is the harsh reminder of man's arrogant presumption (Gen. 3:3). God has the last word. Tillich defines anxiety as "the self-awareness of the finite self as finite."[7] In keeping with our findings, it seems preferable to alter the definition to read: "the self-awareness of the finite self as *fallen.*" It is not simply human restriction, but alienation and degradation which trouble man. He has responsibility without rectitude. Introspection suggests his anxiety, and his social relationships confirm it.

It is no doubt significant that Freud observed anxiety to precede repression: "To our astonishment, the result was the reverse of what we had expected. It is not repression that creates anxiety: it is there first and creates repression."[8] In other words, anxiety does not come as the result of man's using a psychological defense mechanism, but rather anxiety is a pre-condition for them. Anxiety is a state of being rather than a condition to which the individual responds. For its significance we must defer to inference and/or revelation. Kierkegaard stressed the anticipatory factor of decision, and Tillich the realization of finiteness. The more inclusive and accurate description seems to be that anxiety is the characteristic experience of responsible but fallen man.

GOD NOT ABSENTED

Although man is alienated from God, Yahweh has not absented himself (vs. 2). *Deo absente* is the condition of hell, but not of this life. The world and affairs of man continue to be sustained by common grace—God's favor extended to all mankind. God sits in silence, surveying the scene of man's abhorrent practice, and listening to man's self-incriminations. His person is unaltered in holiness, and His righteous purpose for man is unchanged.

What does alienated man understand of God's presence? God is said to be known to man, so that he is without excuse (Rom.

[7]Paul Tillich, *Systematic Theology*, I, p. 192.
[8]Sigmund Freud, *New Introductory Lectures on Psychoanalysis*, p. 120.

1:19-20). This fact has led to seemingly endless speculation. Are
there formal arguments which can demonstrate God's existence?
The very use of such arguments seems rather to point to a difficulty in perception. Probably, alienated man's awareness of God
is more fundamental and inclusive than the theistic arguments
might imply. As Borden P. Bowne has said: "Thesim is not
explicit in anything, but implicit in everything." God is the
numinous, the *other* in man's experience. Man explains the *numinous* in various ways, but he can never really escape the awareness of God's presence.

Man banishes God from his consciousness (vs. 1). He is remarkably equipped with defense mechanisms to accomplish God's
demise. He *represses*—excluding his experiences with God from
conscious awareness; he *projects*—attributing to other people and/
or situations the problems resulting from his alienation from God;
he *introjects*—borrowing the esteem of others for himself; and he
rationalizes—creating good reasons for his bad actions. One can
speculate on the effects such defense mechanisms have on the
personality of alienated man. Psychologist James Murray believes
that it is not without serious personal disorder: "*A priori*, the
thwarting of a mind in its desire for God, even though that
thwarting, as so often happens with other instincts, be half or
wholly conscious, must produce serious consequences."[9] The
psalmist's elaboration of man's symptomatic ills may be an indication of the price man pays for disregarding God (vss. 1-4).

The poet affirms God's presence (vs. 2), and the fact that it is
manifest in human events (vs. 5). His train of thought is abruptly
broken by the word "there," as if some incident were meant to
demonstrate God's involvement. The parallel passage in Psalm 53
adds: "For God has scattered the bones of him that encamps
against you. You have put (them) to shame, because God has
despised them." A deliverance of God's people from the enemy
is clearly implied. Pharaoh's harsh oppression of Israel was tolerated for a period, but then plagues fell upon the land and the
Egyptian army was overturned in the sea. Sennacherib's army
appeared invincible in its conquests, but it was humbled in God's

[9]James Murray, *An Introduction to Christian Psycho-Therapy*, p. 90.

time. There is no simple correlation between evil act and re-compense (vs. 2), but righteousness is vindicated in due season (vs. 5). Viewed by man, judgment breaks suddenly, but God's moral purpose with man is never altered or relaxed.

Alienated man is reminded of God's presence not only by event but by person (vs. 6). The humble *(anah)* may be those subdued by the oppressor, but more likely they are those who humble themselves before God. They put their trust in Yahweh, who is their confidence and refuge. The fool's effort to discredit them by ridicule and impiety fails. Their witness is more persistent and less capable of being ignored than the judgment which is periodically openly displaced in the fall of an Epiphanes or a Hitler. The changing fortunes of life, far from stilling the voice of the humble, cause faith to ring with clarion assurance.

The fool will not recognize God, but he cannot escape Him. Through historical events, by the witness of the redeemed, the Almighty awakens man to the reality which he tries desperately to repress—that God is present. The Hound of Heaven allows man no hiding place. Man's anxiety results then, not merely from his finiteness but from the fact that he is a frustrated fugitive.

At this point the psalm drops the consideration of man in futile flight in order to contrast it with the abiding confidence of Yahweh's people (vs. 7). In verse 7 we have most likely an idiomatic reference to captivity, a response for the suffering faithful of all generations. Deliverance from an enemy is but a temporary respite for God's folk, but His grace sustains them through all eventualities. In either case, what is testing for the humble is testimony to the fool.

CONCLUSION

Man is thoroughly corrupted, the ideal defaced. The funda-mental nature of his defection is hinted at by the extent of his depravity. His violation of theonomous law has resulted in aliena-tion from God and moral degradation. Man looked for liberty but found bondage; he searched for life but experienced death.

In flight from God, man only succeeds in losing himself and experiences a state of profound uncertainty which gives rise to anxiety. His sins are symptomatic of his fallen situation.

Reform, the rejection of past sins, and catharsis, alleviation of anxiety, fail to get at the root problem. The psalm leaves us considering the fool—compounding his estrangement by thought and deed; the faithful—periodically encouraged by an event but always sustained by grace; and God—refusing to leave man to his self-destruction.

⊨⊐ *3* ⊏⊨

About Face

⊢━━━━━⊐⊏━━⊐⊏━━━━━⊣

The psalmist describes his . . . life [after conversion]. It consists fundamentally of the fact that God has forgiven him. . . . The complex of negative attitudes which had crippled him are replaced by confidence in God's purpose no matter how his life circumstances may alter. This experience is less the power of positive thinking than the practice of realistic perception. Faith is not in faith but in God, not in a pragmatic means for mental health but in the redemptive purpose of the Almighty.

About Face

A psalm of David, Maskil.

1. Blessed is he whose transgression is forgiven, whose error is covered.
2. Blessed is the man to whom Yahweh reckons no perverseness, and in whose spirit there is no deception.
3. When I kept silence, my body wasted away, through my groaning all through the day. *grief — as Wayne lives when nil stopped*
4. Because day and night Your hand was heavy upon me; my moisture was evaporated by the summer. Selah. *made up hard deception*
5. I made known my errors to You, and did not hide my perverseness. I said that I would confess my transgressions unto Yahweh, and You forgave the perversity of my error. Selah.
6. For this shall all the godly pray unto You at a time when You can be found. In the flood of great waters, they shall not reach him.
7. You are a hiding place to me, You preserve me from trouble, You encompass me with deliverance. Selah.
8. I will instruct you and enlighten you in the way you should go, I will counsel you with My eye upon you. *his advice to other after his*
9. Do not be like a horse or mule, without understanding, held with bit and bridle in order that they do not come near you. *trouble over what he learned from it*
10. Numerous are the sorrows of the wicked, but he who trusts in Yahweh, mercy shall surround him.
11. Be glad in Yahweh, rejoice you righteous, and cry for joy all you who are upright in heart.

PSALM 32

42

God intended man to be a person, with all the fulfillment implied by that term. However, selfhood is contingent upon rectitude, involving a right relationship with his Creator and his fellow man, and these conditions of his being have been violated. He is homo alienatus—*alienated man. There is still in him the capacity for knowing God, but communion is lacking. He senses responsibility, but no longer perceives its nature or realizes its function. Anxiety plagues the frustration of his ego ideal.*

God has not vacated His creation. He is present, revealing Himself in providential acts and through the faith of His people. His revelation has a redemptive purpose (John 3:17). He wants to bring man to Himself—Yahweh—and in so doing to himself—authentic man.

There are seemingly an endless number of home remedies for man's restoration. Their success is limited and for this reason deceptive. The psalmist empties the medicine cabinet in favor of God's prescription. He describes the basis, suggests the means, and extends the offer of restoration.

GROUND OF RESTORATION

The most striking thing about the text is that God takes the initiative in restoring man, rather than encouraging man to do something by himself (vs. 2). In other words, restoration is the result of grace (unmerited favor) rather than works which is merit by deed. The opening verses elaborate this theme. The three terms depicting God's initiative correspond to those suggesting man's hopeless plight.

1. God forgives *(nasá)* man (vs. 1). The parallel term is transgression *(pesha)*, a violation of divine commandment. It implies passing over a prescribed boundary or participating in the forbidden thing. The term for forgiveness means to lift away, as if to relieve one of his iniquity.

2. God covers *(kasah)* man's sin (vs. 1). The corresponding word is error *(chataah)*, the failure to realize the natural aim or pur-

pose of life. It is missing the mark. *Kasah* is employed of God's covering the deep with the waters (Psa. 104:6), and the heavens with clouds (Psa. 147:8). It was commonly used in connection with the sacrifices, when man's defilement was covered by the application of blood.

6. God reckons *(chashab)* no sin to man (vs. 2). Perversity *(avon)* suggests turning aside from the proper course, taking a crooked way. The extent as well as the nature of man's offense is implied, as illustrated in the later phrase, "the perversity (iniquity) of my error" (vs. 5). God does not hold man's sin against him; the offense is canceled.

This passage on man's plight and God's provision finds its way into Paul's discussion of the divine program for reclamation (Rom. 4:7-8). The immediate subject is justification *(dikaiosis)*, a forensic or legal concept. The man justified is declared in harmony with the law's demands. Negatively, pardon of the offender is involved: "There is therefore now no condemnation of those who are in Christ Jesus" (Rom. 8:1). Positively, there is access to God (Rom. 5:1-2), adoption-birth (Rom. 8:15-16), and life eternal (Rom. 5:21; 6:22; 8:29-30).

Before proceeding further, we should point out that grace does not imply an indiscriminate bestowal of God's favor. The psalmist describes the man accepted by God as one whose spirit is purged of insincerity (vs. 2). There is no justification of the sinner without judgment of the sin. Justification means not only forgiveness of the death penalty, but a new life in Christ (Rom. 5:18; 6:4, 6, 23). The believer is freed from the dominion of sin (Rom. 5:20; 6:7), and empowered to live unto God (Rom. 5:5, 15-17; 6:2, 4-11). Grace does not lay aside the consideration of moral law, but makes it possible to keep that law. Paul adds that a continuing obedience is necessary to experience the victory of God in daily life (Rom. 6:12-20).

Why is grace necessary to man's restoration? The question is not easy to answer. The clue seems to be in the nature of theonomous law, as it reflects the nature of God and as it bears on man's character. The language of relationship may assist in understanding the issue: "True forgiveness is only possible when the wronged person experiences the hurt or wound to his live sentiment, overcomes the inevitable sense of alienation created between him and the wrong-doer, and identifies himself with the wrong-doer as though the sin were his own."[1] We believe that while God may be personal in some distinctive sense, He is not radically other than that which we mean by personality. In our own experience we have learned that openness to another means that we feel the pain of wrong done to us. There is no true forgiveness without hurt, but hurt does not necessarily end in forgiveness. The sense of injury is the opportunity for forgiveness—if the subject overcomes the sense of alienation and identifies himself with the other in his sin. This is grace. This is what God has done in the face of man's defection.

Man cannot forgive himself. It is not his prerogative to do so. He cannot have fellowship with God until and unless God stands with him. The good news is that God *has* identified with man, taking his sin as if it were His own (II Cor. 5:21).

Theonomous law calls our attention not only to God, but to the moral nature of man. Carroll Wise's clinical insight is helpful at this point. He distinguishes disease—a physical ailment—from illness—a negative response of the person to his condition or situation. Illness, then, is a process involving feelings and attitudes. By this definition, diphtheria is a disease and alcoholism is an illness. Reproach or appeal is an ineffective means of restoring the ill. Rather, we must first "discover the conditions out of which the illness arose. Next, we have to find ways to reverse these conditions and their effect on the body or mind or on our total being. Then we have to discover ways of continuing to live so that the conditions creating illness are not repeated."[2]

God's grace works in a similar fashion. Law demands that man function appropriately, but grace makes it possible for him to do so. In this way, and only in this way, is man to be renewed.

Man cannot cure himself. A ganglion of perverse feelings and attitudes incapacitates him. Grace frees him to consider the conditions from which his difficulty arose, and the means to reverse the situation and sustain new-found health.

---

[1] John McKenzie, *Guilt, Its Meaning and Significance*, p. 160.
[2] Carroll Wise, *Mental Health and the Bible*, p. 4.

CONTEXT FOR RESTORATION

The psalm now takes a distinctively autobiographical turn (vs. 3). The poet tells of the inner torment which preceded forgiveness. His guilt is expressed in vivid metaphor, in order to stress the intensity of the experience and the folly of resisting God.

Guilt

The author tells us that his body ached with anguish, and groans escaped his lips (vs. 3) like those of a suffering animal. There was no articulation, only torment given breath. But for all the pain, he would not confess his sin.

Guilt must be distinguished from feeling guilty. Scripture encourages a realistic appraisal of guilt. As an example, Christ customarily pricked the self-righteous religious leaders (Matt. 23:13-33), and consoled the ostracized (Luke 19:1-10). He made a point of correcting improper guilt feelings (Luke 15:11-32).

There are times when guilt is the appropriate feeling. If one commits murder without pangs of conscience, something is wrong. In fact, man's ability to anticipate the feeling of guilt is a preventative against an evil course of action. Guilt feelings sent by God are specific, based on man's transgression. True guilt is consciously focused on the offense, rather than festering in a nebulous fashion in the subconscious. It locates guilt feelings in sin instead of creating reasons to satisfy guilt feelings.

Man's sin lies not only in specific infractions of the law but in the nature of defection itself. Christ's response to the news of the Galileans who perished at Pilate's hand is an excellent commentary (Luke 13:1-3). The people had supposed this to be a special visitation of God's wrath in judgment on sin, but Christ answered: "No, but except you repent, you shall all likewise perish." He reinforced the point by referring to a similar disaster resulting from the fall of Siloam's tower (Luke 13:4-5). All men are guilty of breaking theonomous law. But these infractions which vary from person to person and with an individual from time to time, fade into relative insignificance compared to man's rejection of himself before God.

We may safely say that all men experience guilt feelings. They stem in part from such early childhood experiences as toilet training, correction for handling an erotic area of the body, or weaning from breast-feeding. They are multiplied by the family and societal mores with which the youth must cope, and even an adult is only in a relative fashion able to handle guilt feelings constructively. The feelings are painful, potentially destructive, and not to be induced indiscriminately. The Scripture's stress on guilt is realistic, related both to specific transgressions of and existential defection from God's law.

Guilt promoted by God has a purpose. Immanuel Kant provocatively observed: "Fear of God is not rooted in his Holiness and goodness, but in His unerring justice."[3] It is the realization that divine judgment is perfect justice which intensifies guilt (Gal. 6:7-8); and so the psalmist felt God's hand pressed down heavily and without respite (vs. 4). His bones ached from the pressure, and his vitality was dissipated like moisture from the body under a scorching sun. To use a colloquial expression, God "leaned on" him."

The fear of God is the beginning of wisdom (Psa. 111:10; Prov. 9:10). For years I thought that Christians were hedging by making a distinction between *fear* and *reverence*. Then it occurred to me that fear as it is generally understood causes man to flee, while reverence is intended to draw man (Psa. 115:11). Guilt is not intended to induce despair but to provide hope.

Guilt is preparation, an introduction to grace. It is the internal stress which reminds man of his need. Guilt is to be welcomed, for while "it can no doubt be 'a fearful thing to fall into the hands of the living God' (Heb. 10:31), . . . it is a worse thing to fall out of them."[4] The psalmist was in an enviable position compared to the calloused and arrogant devourer of God's people (Psa. 14:4, 5).

There is no merit to guilt *per se*, but only in its insistence that human ills be treated. Whoever revels in guilt is sick; whoever

[3]Immanuel Kant, *Lectures on Ethics*, p. 97.
[4]J. R. P. Sclater, *The Interpreter's Bible*, IV, p. 170.

ignores guilt is stupid; whoever learns from guilt is wise. When guilt has led man to God, it has fulfilled its divine mission.

Grace

The psalmist determines to conceal his sin no longer, but confesses it openly before God (vs. 5). This amounts to life's turning, an about-face or conversion *(strepho)*. Unlike proselytism, implying an external adherence, conversion suggests a basic life reorientation. One repents of the previous course of action and optimistically undertakes the new.

Repentance is sorrow for one's past action, coupled with the sincere desire to forsake that pattern of behavior. The man who turns to God, turns from sin. It is the Almighty's intent to save man *from* rather than *in* sin. Remorse over sin is not enough. Rejection of sin, feeble though man's resolve may be, is the necessary element which distinguishes a Peter from a Judas.

Confidence in the new life is generally expressed by the words "trust" *(batach*—to lean upon; *chasah*—to take refuge in; *peitho*—to be persuaded of) and "faith" *(pistis*—to remain steadfast). It is a personal commitment, the total response of man to the gracious invitation of God.

Faith may be singled out as an especially suggestive term, one rich with meaning. Its most obvious intent is to express reliance. E. H. Hoffman captures the idea in the words of a gospel song:

> What have I to dread, what have I to fear,
> Leaning on the everlasting arms?
> I have peace complete with my Lord so near,
> Leaning on the everlasting arms.

The idea of reliance must nonetheless be qualified. Faith is childlike, that is trustful, but not childish, that is uncritical (see Rom. 12:2). It is the response of the entire person in whatever stage of developing maturity. The child's faith is not adequate for the adult (I Cor. 13:11) but is not less relevant for the child. The failure to realize this truth is illustrated in the life of the famed writer Eugene O'Neill. As a man he rejected the experience of a young student of the catechism, but was unable to replace it with a faith appropriate to the man of letters.

Faith is never simply passive. Hebrews 11 describes those prodigious in faith by their exploits. We must weigh works of faith, however, in terms of the subject's health, opportunity, and calling. An equitable appraisal must go beyond mere appearance (John 7:24). A woman I know was terrified at anything that might momentarily eclipse the security of her home. At one point she claimed a spiritual victory by sitting on her porch while the door was ajar. She was a tormented and emotionally crippled person, but one with great faith.

The accomplishment of faith is also conditioned by opportunity. A troubled youth approached me with a problem at the close of one worship service. He indicated that he had the qualifications to excel as a preacher, but his lack of education disqualified him from being considered by the church officials. The confidence was not lacking, but the occasion to demonstrate it was absent. Likely, the better indication of faith would have been his willingness to undertake a prescribed course of preparation. On the other hand, the preaching ministry might not have been God's purpose for the young man. I suspect that it was not. Christian fruitfulness is not limited to, or necessarily best illustrated by, the church vocation field. Faith knows no such boundaries.

Incidentally, Christ promised astounding results from infinitesimal faith (Matt. 17:20). C. S. Lewis puts the same idea in a more restrained Western manner of speaking: "The smallest good act today is the capture of a strategic point from which, a few months later, you may be able to go on to victories you never dreamed of."[5] The believer faithfully struggles for *high ground*, a point of advantage from which a further assault can be launched.

We may now give more direct consideration to the experience of conversion. The whole man is the subject of conversion, although its effects may be realized primarily and/or more immediately in one area or another. As an indication of the diversity, Owen Brandon analyzes conversion as dominantly intellectual, emotional, or moral (volitional):

[5]C. S. Lewis, *Mere Christianity*, p. 102.

1. *Intellectual*—the acceptance of a new idea, or a new understanding of an old idea: in this case the conversion is characterized by a process of mental enlightenment and of spiritual understanding; or
2. *Emotional*—the birth of a new and dominating affection; the subject feels constraint by the love of God, and responds in love to God: in this case the conversion is characterized by a reorganization of the emotional life around this new center; or
3. *moral*—the confession of failure: a reorientation of the will in respect of its dominant aim for life.[6]

Man is converted to God. The functional principles by which this is achieved have been described as repentance and faith or trust. The instrumental means by which man is converted is Christ's redemptive work. He is the sole mediator (I Tim. 2:5), the effective priest and perfect offering (Heb. 9:13-14), and the very nature of God (Phil. 2:6). "A Christian conversion always and of necessity has the message of Christ as its *psychic conditio sine qua non*."[7]

To believe in Christ is to have faith in the Christ of history. The truth of the incarnation is that God entered into space-time in the person of Christ. The Christ of faith cannot be separated from the Christ of history.

Belief is not simply historic in nature but confessional. It places confidence not only in an historical person, but in one who was incarnate Deity (Phil. 2:7-8). It is assured that the bold claims of Christ are supported by His incomparable character, His unique insight, His mighty acts, and His triumph over death.

"Supposing He was the Son of God, is basic Christianity merely an acquiescence in this truth? No. Once persuaded of the deity of Christ's person, we must examine the nature of His work."[8] Simply put, Christ has reconciled man to God in His life and death. His work is vicarious—acting on our behalf; and it is efficacious—having the power to produce the intended effect.

[6]Owen Brandon, *The Battle for the Soul*, p. 34.
[7]Svene Norborg, *Varieties of Christian Experience*, p. 189.
[8]John R. W. Stott, *Basic Christianity*, p. 8.

Reconciliation is achieved by God but must be appropriated by man.

Theism postulates a personal God, and implies the ability of God to reveal Himself to man. Christianity professes that God has done so in the person of Christ. Theism connotes a God who is concerned for the welfare of man. Christianity affirms that God has demonstrated that concern by bearing man's sin at Calvary, reconciling man to Himself. Faith, then, is faith in the act of God in history, and is consummated in personal appropriation.

We have defined the functional principle of conversion as repentance and faith, and the instrumental means as Christ's vicarious work. To these must be added the efficient organ of conversion, regeneration by God's Spirit. Regeneration or new birth (polingenesia) describes invasion by divine Personality. It stresses the restoration of spiritual vitality which was lost to man in his defection, and prohibited to him in his alienation. Regeneration reminds us that reconciliation is not simply a formal transaction, but access to God's grace and power. Ernest White describes the dynamics of regeneration at some length:

> First of all there is a continual movement of suppression going on to repression. Older habits and desires gradually sink below the level of consciousness. Things which were once attractive and important lose their emotional content, and there is a redirection of affect . . . into new paths of activity . . . . The individual becomes God-centered instead of self-centered . . . the libido is withdrawn from one set of objects and re-attached to new objects and pursuits. A new ideal is set up, an ideal whose center and aim is Christ . . . . This new orientation of the ego ideal is accompanied by a change in the superego. The conscience becomes at once more sensitive and more rational.[9]

We may see from this analysis that the term *new birth* is not too radical a designation.

Repentance, faith, conversion, and regeneration are best thought of as occurring together in man's experience. One does

---

[9]Ernest White, *Christian Life and the Unconscious*, p. 57.

not leave an old way (repentance) until he pursues a new goal (faith). Conversion describes reversal from an old course of action, and regeneration the beginning of a new life. The fundamental change is further stressed by the contrasts between death and life (Eph. 2:1), and darkness and light (John 3:19-21).

Godliness

Can Christianity be true and the disciple false? What of the disparity between profession and practice? We shall want to consider this question in several contexts, but for now it will suffice to characterize the new life. If variance exists, it should be understood in connection with the experience promised, rather than some ambiguous and/or impractical ideal.

After conversion, what may be expected? The psalmist describes his subsequent life (vss. 6-7). It consists fundamentally of the fact that God has forgiven him. Otherwise he would be immobilized by old guilts. He finds that he can forgive himself because God has forgiven him. He conceives of himself as one-who-trusts-in-God, a recipient of God's grace. The complex of negative attitudes which had crippled him are replaced by confidence in God's purpose no matter how his life circumstances may alter.

This experience is less the power of positive thinking than the practice of realistic perception. Faith is not in faith but in God, not in a pragmatic means for mental health but in the redemptive purpose of the Almighty. It does not hope for that which is invalid, but holds on to that which is true.

There are important conditions to keep in mind. God has forgiven, but the scars of old sins remain to vex man. Their results are personal, affecting his physical and mental health, and social, influencing the continuing relationships with others. They are internal, caused by sin's effect on life, and external, reflecting the continuity of his fellows' old estimation of him.

Conversion is not an absolute break with the past, and it does not immunize one against the present. It is no panacea for man's difficulties. The waters still swell at his feet (vs. 6). The difference does not rest in a change of circumstances, but in the potential to face them. The godly person is not saved *out* of the world but *in* it. Appropriately, he is admonished to pray (vs. 6).

The convert can succumb to temptation. George Coe defines such a lapse as "failure on the part of the individual convert to achieve full integration with, and conformity to, the new pattern of life, so that he returns to his former way of living."[10] It follows that backsliding should be interpreted as failure rather than futility. The response to failure should be contrition for one's own sin, and compassion from one's fellow believers.

The testimony of the godly relates to both forgiveness, the setting aside of sin's penalty, and sustenance, the realization of victory over sin's power. The psalmist tells of shelter, preservation through trouble, and deliverance from affliction (vs. 7). The idea is succinctly captured by Paul: "I can do all things through Christ who strengthens me" (Phil. 4:13). Paul was not boasting idly. He was painfully aware of his frailty. Similarly the psalmist recalls the need of prayer (vs. 6).

The godly person affirms God's forgiveness and deliverance. He sees all obstacles, personal and otherwise, against the backdrop of God's sufficiency. The godly life is by definition: "the life entrusted to and trusting in God."

INVITATION TO RESTORATION

Who the speaker is in the remaining verses is not certain (vss. 8-11); it may be either the author as God's prophet or God Himself. In either case, we may understand the passage as a gracious invitation to man.

God's word is gospel—good news. It is proclamation—the report of reconciliation (vss. 1-2), and promise—the pledge to direct a man's way (vs. 8). Yahweh will *instruct*, as if to provide the formal principles for behavior, and *enlighten*, that is, counsel in the application of the principles to given situations. God's moral law acts as the guideline for ethical decisions and His Spirit assists the believer in reaching decisions consistent with these norms.

Man is offered not only the promise but the presence of the

---

[10]George A. Coe, *The Psychology of Religion*, p. 71.

Almighty, which is the significance intended by reference to "My eye" (vs. 8). Alienated man suffers from existential loneliness—the isolation resulting from his sin. It is to be distinguished from natural loneliness which is due to circumstance, and irrational loneliness which is a free-floating feeling of exclusion. The acclaim of others provides no continuing respite from the condition. The crowd even has a peculiar way of accentuating the feeling of loneliness. God's invitation establishes immediate rapport with man's need.

No immunity from natural loneliness is promised, and we may suppose that none of us is so healthy of mind as to completely escape irrational loneliness, but God's presence precludes existential loneliness. Christ could testify: "Behold, an hour is coming and has come for you to be scattered each to his own and to leave Me alone [natural loneliness], and yet I am not alone, because the Father is with Me" [absence of existential loneliness] (John 16: 32). The call of God separates individuals from their closest fellows (Matt. 10:34-36), only to reunite them in a ministry of compassion (Matt. 10:42). The first association depends on personal preference, while the latter is a universally available relationship. To choose to stay with our old preferred associates results in an inevitable loss of life, but to respond to God's call brings certain gain (Matt. 10:39). God graciously invites man to relinquish what he cannot hold, in order to gain what he cannot lose.

The promise is followed by a sharp warning (vs. 9). Man is likened to an impervious horse or obstinate mule. He ignores the spoken word until he feels the pull of the bridle and the cut of the bit. The path of righteousness requires discipline, rigor, and persistence. Man shrinks from the challenge, turns to idle pastime, and strays through perversity. If he will not respond to the word of exhortation, he may expect the bridle of correction. There is no pain so intense as that of the believer who has left the way of God.

The invitation is to leave sin. Liberty construed as license is a mockery of God. Grace calls man to responsibility commensurate with its provision. The power of the Almighty is set against the unwilling and stubborn, but is available to the understanding and pliable.

An encouragement succeeds the warning (vss. 10-11). God's will is not disagreeable (Matt. 11:29-30). The way of the wicked is attended with many sorrows, but the godly has every mercy extended to him (vs. 10). Man may respond to God's warning with overcaution, fearfulness, and disabling anxiety; but the psalmist encourages him to openness and joy in the Lord. The thought is beautifully expressed in the purpose of Christ's coming: "For God sent not the Son into the world in order to condemn the world, but that the world might be saved through Him" (John 3:17). God is not only *with* but *for* man.

The invitation is both to life and to abundant living—a fullness implied in verse 11. We shall want to reflect at more length on this subject at a later point. Here we can only point out in passing that the joy of the upright builds to a crescendo: from inward happiness, to outward rejoicing, and even to ecstatic enthusiasm. There is the exaltation of a soul set free. The enthusiasm often more than the logic of the new life commends the invitation to one's fellows.

SUMMARY

God has not banished His alienated creature but has purposed his restoration: forgiveness of violation, covering of sin, and non-reckoning of perversity. His offer of grace is no compromise with sin. The moral law is not set aside but is embodied in God's redemptive plan (Matt. 5:17). The Holy Spirit identifies guilt in connection with man's sin and impending judgment, and offers grace through Christ (John 16:8-11).

While reconciliation is grounded in God's forgiveness and grace, it is man whose way must be altered. Man, rather than God, does an about face. We have analyzed this conversion by suggesting three aspects: the functional—involving man's repentance of evil and trust in God's promise; the instrumental—Christ's vicarious atonement; and the efficient—regeneration by the Holy Spirit. The believer reckons his former life dead with Christ (Rom. 6:9), alive to God through Him (Rom. 6:11), and his life to be yielded as an instrument of righteousness (Rom. 6:13).

The true evangelist is a bringer of good news. He may identify the meaning of anxiety, explain the constructive role of guilt, and remind of the sorrows of wickedness, but his essential message is that God offers reconciliation through His Son. God's purpose is to bring man to fellowship with Him—reconciliation—and fullness of authentic life—restoration. God wants to sweep away the darkness with light, and replace weeping with joy. The tragedy of human experience is countered with the triumph of Christ. Restoration is no further away than proclamation and the whispered response of faith.

4

The Authentic Life

Godliness is not gooeyness, a naïve sentimentality which fails to perceive the nature and demands of spiritual struggle. While admitting that moral judgments are seldom if ever a case of white and black, we must not conclude that all shades of gray are the same. The Christian discriminates, not hesitating to take a stand on the best judgment which informed understanding can render, and to pay the cost of personal involvement.

The Authentic Life

1. Blessed is the man who walks not in the counsel of the wicked, nor stands in the way of sinners, nor sits in the seat of the scornful.
2. But surely his delight is in the law of Yahweh, and in the law he meditates day and night.
3. And he is like a tree planted by the streams of water, which yields fruit in its season, and its leaf does not wither, and whatever he does prospers.
4. The wicked are not like this, but surely are like chaff which the wind drives away.
5. Therefore, the wicked shall not stand in the judgment, nor sinners in the congregation of righteous.
6. Because Yahweh knows the way of the righteous, but the way of the wicked is destruction.

PSALM 1

1. Why do the nations cause an uproar, and the people babble vanity?
2. The kings of the earth set themselves, and the rulers counsel together against Yahweh and His anointed:
3. "Let us break their bands apart, and cast their cords from us."
4. He that sits in the heavens will laugh. The Lord will deride them.
5. Then He will speak to them in His wrath, and afflict them in His fury:
6. "Yet, I have established my king upon Zion, my holy mount."
7. I shall declare as a precept (that) Yahweh said to me: "You are my son, today I have given you birth.
8. "Ask from me, and I will give the nations (as) your inheritance, and the ends of the earth (as) your possession.

9. "You will break them with a rod of iron. As a potter's vessel you will smash them."
10. Now therefore, be wise, you kings; be admonished, you rulers of the earth.
11. Serve Yahweh with fear and rejoice with trembling.
12. Kiss the son, that he be not angry, and you perish (from) the way, for his wrath is easily kindled. Blessed are all who trust in him.

PSALM 2

While the Christian may have the potential for realizing life's purpose, a preliminary question arrests our attention: "What, if at all, does natural man realize of his need for authentic life?" The answer seems to be that he senses an unrealized ideal, but is less than certain of its nature. This is seen in the criticism that Jung "holds out to man the hope that he will become his 'true self', but he can offer a man no account of what that 'true self' will be like ... and more important, that it will be worth while when it is reached."[1]

The first two psalms in the psalter may be considered together as we approach the topic of the authentic life. There is good precedent for this, as shown in the Talmud: " 'Happy is the man,' and 'why are the nations in an uproar' form one psalm," and: "He began with 'Happy,' as it is written, 'Happy is the man' and he terminated with 'Happy,' as it is written, 'happy are all they that take refuge in Him.' "[2] These psalms are thought to constitute an introduction to the Psalter, and we may further consider them as a prologue to the Christian life.

---

[1] David Cox, *op. cit.*, p. 344.
[2] *Berakoth*, 9b. *The Babylonian Talmud.*

CONSTRUCTING THE CASE

There are two kinds of men, the godly (goodly) and the ungodly. The former prosper, while the latter waste away. The Hebrew realized that experience at times seems to belie this revelation. It was for him a troubled but nonetheless persisting confidence.

How are we then to understand the division of mankind into two groups diametrically opposed in terms of their nature and course of life? I believe the resolution may be approached through the concepts of *differentiation* and *distillation*. The former refers to the means by which we qualify more precisely the complex nature of things.

A young friend of mine had had four arrests by the time he was twelve. How many other times he had violated the law is open to speculation. I sat in the judge's chamber with him as the court official attempted to unravel the incredibly confused factors which contributed to the lad's warfare against society. Slowly and painfully certain things concerning his relationship to his home and his peer group came to light. This is an example of differentiation.

Distillation is the opposite of differentiation. It is the means by which a subject is condensed to its essential nature. To continue the illustration used of differentiation, the judge had to reach a decision concerning my friend. His disposition of the case had to be based on the trend of the boy's behavior as it might be modified by corrective efforts. So we may understand the contrast between godly and ungodly man as the distillation of life to its basic nature. This does not negate differentiation—the complex personal and societal factors which affect man's behavior—but interprets it in the light of theonomous law.

Analysis

The psalmist characterizes authentic existence in two ways: negatively as not perpetuating alienation from God (vs. 1), and positively as delighting in and motivated by His law (vs. 2). It is, in a phrase, "the godly life."

Godliness is not the same as being God. It is an attribute not of man's nature but of his relationship to Another. The inescapable snare of failing to recognize this distinction is self-righteousness, the supposition that one has an intrinsic worth which guarantees his moral superiority.

The problem does not reside here so far as the Christian's associates are concerned. They have no difficulty in distinguishing him from God. But they do have difficulty seeing a marked difference from themselves. The fact is that no such distinction is clearly and consistently evident. We may suppose that the reason for this is that goodness reflects harmony within the individual and between persons, as well as with God. Reconciliation does not disregard the poor traits of character which have been years and, in a sense, ages in the making. A man's spiritual progress cannot be measured against his fellows, but is *clued* by his new life orientation and alteration of life from the old pattern.

The Christian is also aware of the disparity between the will of God and his own way of life. He is tempted to morbid reflection, and inordinate sensitivity at this point. He builds up a peculiar ambivalence in regard to his self-image; he is somehow saved by God's grace but is hardly affected as a result. He gives himself away in his testimony which speaks of God's grace in an impersonal fashion, and reeks with self-disparagement. The unfortunate result is joylessness.

Depreciation does not, any more than pride, adequately reflect man as the recipient of God's favor. Both may be thought of as perpetuating the image of death (vs. 1), rather than life (vs. 2). Both demonstrate an obsession with self and a failure to see oneself realistically as godly.

The practical question remains, however: How does one put aside the body of death and take up the image of life? Paul's counsel is applicable here: "Even so reckon yourselves to be dead to sin but alive to God in Christ Jesus" (Rom. 6:11). We are urged to consider the implication of reconciliation, the result of turning from the wages of sin to the way of God. To be sure, the reflection is marred by disparity from the ideal, but the Christian does not presume total achievement, a goal which inevitably must elude finite man. He is prone to sin and requires repentance and restoration; but the distillation of his life is that he is godly, sustained by divine fellowship.

The Christian not only considers the implication of reconciliation, but places confidence in the blessing of God. The man is blessed fully, or most blessed, who does not take the sinner's way. Here must be the confidence. The world fears that Christ will rob it of some pleasure, some rewarding life experience. It is therefore natural that His claims be suspect and His guidance rejected. The believer, on the other hand, has concluded that he has been accepted into the household of faith, and that Christ is the source of strength, joy, and life itself.

The transformation of man's self-image also depends on a contrast with the stubborn: "Happy is the man who does not walk in the disposition cherished by the ungodly, who is still further from associating in the vicious life of sinners, or from having delight in the society of scoffers at religion."[3] The verbs (walk, stand, sit), describe the successive steps of the evil life, progressive confirmation in wickedness. They begin with a subtle adoption of the wrong principles, followed by a persisting practice of offenses, and end with a deliberate and open mocking of the Almighty. The momentum of the wicked way increases until all restraint is thrown aside and man jeers at God in his evil abandonment. There is implied here not simply a judgment of the impious but a counsel to the godly. The good man is *not* like this. He must not entertain such thoughts. Subtle as they are, these attitudes will eventuate in his destruction (vs. 1).

Rather, the blessed man gives himself deliberately to meditation on God's law (vs. 2). The psalmist feels no contradiction in setting his affection on the law, as though it would result in idolatry. To esteem the law is to respect the Giver. Only when the law is employed in juxtaposition to God is man endangered. The elusive but necessary self-image is obtained by considering the implication of reconciliation, by confidence in the gracious course of godliness in contrast to the impervious determination of the wicked, and by celebration of the word of God.

---

[3]Delitzsch, *op. cit.*, I, p. 111.

The authentic life then, is one of communion with God, enriching a man's capabilities, in contrast to a life of subtle defection, which builds into arrogance and hostility.

Imagery

By his effective use of the image of a vigorous, fruitful tree, the psalmist suggests that the good life consists of growing confidence in the way sustained by God, increasing openness to life's existence as a result, developing fullness of living, and improving function. We shall want to consider these four factors as they relate to the Christian life.

Leaf and fruit are the confident expectation of the man who plants a fruit tree (vs. 3). So the man who says "yes" to the life in God may confidently expect to produce the fruits of that life (Phil. 4:13). A. H. Maslow's description of self-realization could be an account of this experience: "The Freudian 'instincts' and defenses are less sharply set off against each other. The impulses are more expressed and less controlled; the controls are less rigid, inflexible, anxiety-determined. The superego is less harsh and punishing and less set off against the ego. The primary and secondary processes are more equally available and more equally valued."[4] There is an integration of and confidence in life as found through Christ.

The result is a new openness to living. The believer affirms life, rather than denying it. He rides the crest and wake of experience, certain that: "As there is a curse wrapped up in the wicked man's mercies, so there is a blessing concealed in the righteous man's crosses, losses, and sorrows."[5] "No good thing does the Lord withhold from those who walk uprightly" (Psa. 84:11).

Life is as bountiful as the lush foliage of trees by the irrigation waters (vs. 3). Man's roots tap the life-giving source, and his experience responds to the warmth of each day's opportunity. Such life is characterized by spontaneity. Having been planted by

---

[4]A. H. Maslow, "Some Basic Propositions of a Growth and Self Actualization Psychology," *Theories of Personality*, Lindzey and Hall, eds., p. 312.

[5]Charles Spurgeon, *The Treasury of David*, II, pp. 2-3.

the waters of God's law, one has a decreasing feeling of tension or of concern over legislation. The bonds of guilt and preoccupation with failure which had strapped life previously are released to permit abundant living (John 10:10).

The tree that has been planted in the desert waste is still a tree. However, its lack of fruit in season and its dried leaves attest to the poverty of its function (vs. 4). Conversely, the plant by the water's edge is vigorous and productive. "The man who delights in God's Word, being taught by it, bringeth forth patience in the time of suffering, faith in the day of trial, and holy joy in the hour of prosperity."[6] He is not conformed to the accidents of life but rather molds them into the means of grace.

The authentic life does not result automatically (vss. 1-2), nor is it achieved arbitrarily (vs. 4). It comes from deliberate planting by the theonomous waters (vs. 3). Put in other words, the authentic life is not universally realized by man nor grasped by human resolve, but is the revelation and the gift of God.

CHRIST'S COMMENTARY

Jesus Christ gave us a penetrating commentary on the nature of the authentic life as it is lived by the godly man. We are told that Jesus taught His disciples in the presence of the multitude (Matt. 5:1; 7:28). The disciples had left all to follow Him. Their future was as uncertain as their present was precarious. Their resources were limited, and the task great. There was unrest and confusion. For all this, the Lord called them "blessed" in the presence of the multitude, and proceeded to elaborate on aspects of their calling:

The blessed man is poor. The society of Jesus' day knew much social inequality. The rich got richer, and the poor became poorer. The New Testament puts repeated stress on the necessity of assisting those in need (Matt. 9:21, Mark 10:21; Rom. 15:26). The oppression of the poor is singled out by the prophets for condemnation (Amos 4:1; Zech. 7:10; Luke 16:20, 25). While man may neglect them, God does not forget (Psa. 9:18) but delivers

---

[6]*Ibid.,* p. 2.

the poor (Psa. 34:6, 19). The poor *(ptochos)* had become
equated with "those whom God delivers." Matthew adds the
words "in spirit" in order to clarify this point. There is no benefit
attributed to poverty as such. Once loosed from worldly possessions, a man is poor, no matter how rich. No matter how poor, a
man with trust in God is eternally rich.

The blessed man mourns. Mourning *(penthos)* is best taken in
its broadest meaning to imply a general and continual attitude of
the soul, a recognition that no earthly consolation can suffice. It
implies rejection of what the world calls security, the protective
isolation of goods and services. It means identification with the
world in its guilt, weeping for those who have no tears, and fear-
ing for those who lack reverence. "Sorrow cannot tire them or
wear them down, it cannot embitter them or cause them to break
down under the strain: far from it, for they bear their sorrow in
the strength of Him who bears them up, who bore the whole
suffering of the world upon the cross."[7] For all their trials, they
feel a joy for His presence, and the realization that the very
travail of soul is but the birth pangs of a better world.

The blessed man is gentle. Gentle *(praus)* is a many-faceted
word, rich in application. It suggests endurance instead of retalia-
tion, gentleness in preference to abusiveness, honesty in place of
ostentation, meekness in contrast to rowdiness, and mildness as
opposed to bitterness. It is the peculiar self-description of Christ:
"Say to the daughter of Zion, behold your king is coming to you,
gentle and mounted on an ass, even upon a colt, the foal of an ass"
(Matt. 21:5). Understood as an internal frame of mind, humility
is a fair synonym. The gentle man is no more self-effacing than
he is self-pretentious. He is not conscious of being humble, but
rejoices in the presence of God and the vitality of living. As an
external manner of behavior, a good equivalent is pliability. The
gentle man is neither swayed by every change in wind direction,
nor is he bound by tradition, but he is free to take the appropriate
course of action commended by conviction.

The blessed man hungers and thirsts after righteousness. This
figure of speech is most apt, considering the hungry and parched

---

[7]Dietrich Bonhoeffer, *The Cost of Discipleship*, p. 122.

who listened to Jesus. It may also reflect something of the anxiety felt by the disciples over daily provision. The words are not only natural for the occasion but emotive, speaking of a desire so intense as to be painful. Some have thought the words a polemic against the Pharisees and their zeal over the details of tradition (cf. Matt. 5:20). In this light, the intent may be to stress a man's wholehearted response to Christ, as contrasted to a meticulous observance of minutiae.

The blessed man is merciful. The word for merciful, *elias*, is used of God (Eph. 2:4). It includes the idea of compassion (Heb. 2:17) and the desire to remove the evils which excite such feeling. The gentle person bears the injustice of the world, but the merciful addresses himself to the world's need. Both the means by which assistance may be rendered and the willingness to set aside dignity in the course of service are implied in this beatitude.

The blessed man is pure in heart. The concept of *katharos* suggests sincerity as opposed to hypocrisy, and moral blamelessness in contrast to an external show of piety. Paul charged the youth Timothy not to become engaged in obscure speculations, but to heed the charge of love issuing from a pure heart, good conscience, and sincere faith (I Tim. 1:5). Purity seems to imply a rather childlike simplicity. Childlikeness is, as we have noted, not childishness; the former is a resolute confidence coupled with responsible action, while the latter is a retardation to immature ways of behavior.

The blessed man makes peace. Making peace *(eierenapoios)* requires going beyond merely loving peace to the initiation and preservation of peace. The prominent Rabbi Hillel taught: "Be ye of the disciples of Aaron, loving peace and pursuing peace."[8] The man who would make peace must hear complaint on every side, be given to self-control, and be manifestly impartial. He must have the courage of his convictions, the loving tact to apply them, and unswerving patience to see them reach fruition. He will have to reject easy compromise for righteous reconciliation of differences. His own life may be the cost of his effort.

The blessed man is persecuted. The word *diōgmos* means to put

---

[8] *Aboth*, 1:12. *The Babylonian Talmud.*

to flight, to drive away or to pursue, and from this derivation, to persecute. Scripture prickles with the warning of oppression for the disciple (Matt. 10:23; Luke 11:49; Rom. 12:14; I Cor. 4:12). This does not mean that the disciple should search for persecution, or become concerned if he is not experiencing it. The world will bring affliction upon him, and the manner in which it comes is both subtle and insidious. The Christian's concern must be rather that he suffer not as an evildoer, but in the service of God (I Peter 2:20).

The Beatitudes may be thought of as sermons on the theme of the godly man. They are specifically provided as instructions to the disciples who have been called from their many walks of life to follow Christ. They express divergence from the established norms of society, the cost of discipleship, and the consequent happiness. The principles which they convey were personified in Christ. The Beatitudes are but guidelines; one's relationship to Christ is the crux of the issue. They are not so much a list of things to do as aids to the compulsive obedience felt by the disciples. They were also words of comfort which would be so necessary for the difficult days that lay ahead for those first disciples—and which no disciple may avoid. The Beatitudes set the tone for the Christian life; they are the priorities which make life meaningful.

Christ instructed His disciples in the presence of the multitude. His words were an apologetic for the Christian life, a rationale for his course of action. He explained something of the dynamic which the disciple realizes in the process of living out his faith. His appeal has a realistic ring to it; it awakens and joins with man's desire for authentic reality, but it reverberates against his hard resistance to the way of God.

CONTRAST w/ beatitude of

We return to the psalmist for the purpose of extending the contrast between the two ways of life (vss. 4-6). The text is emphatic: "Not so the wicked!" Our concern is with the contrast rather than with elaborating on the state of the perishing. The advantage of the goodly is heightened by the comparison—his life is fruitful instead of barren, rooted and secure instead of unsubstantial (vs. 4).

The godly need not fear the judgment (vss. 5-6). Charles Spurgeon imagines the flight of the wicked from the company of those who stand before God. "Fear shall lay hold upon them there; they shall not stand their ground; they shall fly away; they shall not stand in their own defence; for they shall blush and be covered with eternal contempt."[9] The Christian can comprehend most fully the nature of world-under-divine-judgment. Since he is *in* but not *of* the world, he can feel more intensively the tension over theonomous law. Where the wicked may interpret the day of grace as a guarantee of security, the godly sees it as an indication of God's longsuffering.

CONFLICT

The theme of the godly and wicked is continued in the next psalm. Here the order of treating the subjects is reversed. The psalm falls into four stanzas of three verses each: conduct of the rebellious nations (vss. 1-3), counsel by God (vss. 4-6), claim of the anointed (vss. 7-9), and counsel to the erring (vss. 10-12).

Conduct of the Rebellious Nations

The setting of Psalm 2 seems to be a coronation, accompanied by a threatened uprising (vss. 1-3). Likely encouraged by a new dynasty and the attending difficulties of consolidating authority, the rebels feel secure in their defection. The psalmist turns our view away from the principle of tension between the godly and wicked to its practice, from contrast to conflict.

Authenticity does not preclude but rather demands moral conflict in this life. In the words of Isaac Watts:

> Are there no foes for me to face?
>   Must I not stem the flood?
> Is this vile world a friend to grace,
>   To help me on to God?

---

[9]Spurgeon, *op. cit.*, II, p. 3.

> Sure I must fight, if I would reign.
> Increase my courage, Lord.
> I'll bear the toil, endure the pain,
> Supported by Thy word.

The believer knows no peace in a world where men aim to oppose God's will. For example, the early Christians celebrated the release of Peter and John by quoting this psalm (Acts 4:25-26). They pictured the magistrates as a potent adversary and prayed for boldness to speak and for a demonstration of the Spirit's power (Acts 4:29-30).

Godliness is not gooeyness, a naïve sentimentality which fails to perceive the nature and demands of spiritual struggle. While admitting that moral judgments are seldom if ever a case of white and black, we must not conclude that all shades of gray are the same. The Christian discriminates, not hesitating to take a stand on the best judgment which informed understanding can render, and to pay the cost of personal involvement.

Counter by God   2

Our scene changes from earth to heaven, much in the fashion of the book of Job (vss. 4-6). The transition is grand: from the clamor of earth to the security of heaven, from agitation to resolute confidence. The slow, stately rhythm of the passage suggests the inevitability of God's purpose. He laughs at the futility of His enemies (vs. 4) and follows the derision with a sharp rebuke (vs. 6).

Here we have anthropomorphism of the boldest order, no doubt meant to sharpen the effect. As with such passages, we must interpret the language in relation to the revealed nature of God. He takes no pleasure in striking down those bent with destructive intent, but He will break their counsel in unerring and gratifying justice.

In these verses the godly sees life from the throneroom, viewing evil in its variance from divine justice. He welcomes the abuse of man in preference to disfavor with God (Matt. 10:28). He is in a sense neither worldly, reflecting man's hostility, or otherworldly, removed from the scene of conflict; he is godly, exercising moral conviction in bold involvement with life.

Claim of the Anointed

The heavenly scene fades, making way for the coronation (vss. 7-9). The reign is announced, along with the king's unique relationship to God, his ultimate worldwide authority and complete ascendancy in power. The extravagance of the proclamation outstrips the historical event which provided the original image. The author of Hebrews attributes the words to Jesus (Heb. 1:5; 5:5). The name "My beloved Son" is heard again at Jesus' baptism (Matt. 3:17), and later at the transfiguration (Matt. 17:5; II Peter 1:17-18). Paul relates the decree to the resurrection: "Who was declared to be the Son of God with power by the resurrection" (Rom. 1:3-4), and again: "God has fulfilled this promise to our children in that He raised up Jesus, as it is also written in the Second Psalm 'You are My Son, today I have begotten you' " (Acts 13:33).

Christianity is good news. God stands not only over the world in judgment, but in the world through grace. His Christ (Anointed) is man's Savior. Eternity has touched time with healing.

One might assume that grace would at least minimize the extent of tension, but there seems to be no guarantee that this will happen. The purest expression of God's grace, His own Son, was crucified. It is "the rod of iron" which Christ will take up at His investiture in the end times (Rev. 2:27; 12:5; 19:15), demonstrating man's persisting rejection.

Counsel to the Erring

The final stanza of the psalm is an appeal (vss. 10-12). The two ways are set before man: rebellion against God's Anointed or recognition of His rightful lordship. The tone changes from vivid and exuberant contrasts to a sober and forthright entreaty. The kings and judges are addressed as if to say: "You who have seen the trust of your subjects in regal protection, can you doubt that the man is happy who makes Christ his refuge?" and: "You who provide equity before the law of the land, do you suppose God will be less just?"

The appeal carries the solemn note of solicited reverence (vs.

11). The rabbis taught that even joy should be seasoned with awe. One story went: "Mar the son of Rubina made a marriage feast for his son. He saw that the Rabis were growing very merry, so he brought a cup worth four hundred *zuz* and broke it before them, and they became serious."[10] Not even happiness over God's blessing is to be considered cause for taking Him for granted.

"Blessed are those who trust in Him" (vs. 12). The verse epitomizes the two psalms and is a benediction on the godly. It completes the cycle begun in Psalm 1:1, reminding us that after all, the differentiation of the theme has been accomplished, that in distillation the way of the godly is the path of blessedness.

CONCLUSION

The psalmist was an astute judge of human nature. He would have concurred with A. H. Maslow's statement: "What man needs but does not have, he seeks for unceasingly, and he becomes dangerously ready to jump at any hope, good or bad. The cure for this disease is obvious. We need a validated, usable system of human values that we can believe in and devote ourselves to (be willing to die for), because they are true. . . ."[11]

God's way is good. Accepting His prescription for life results in increased confidence in the way which He sustains, in openness to the varied experiences of this way, in a developing fullness of living, and in a productive service. Paul could confess that all which had seemed important to him previously was nothing in comparison with the life he had found in Christ (Phil. 3:8). The world continues to have difficulty appreciating the felicity of the disciple, not simply because of the irrelevance of creature comforts, but because of the distinctive nature of the redeemed life itself. Yet, Christ did not hesitate to call His followers blessed in the presence of the multitude. They were blessed, not in spite of their calling but because of it.

The Christian is convinced that the events of life illustrate the

[10]*Berakoth*, 30b. *The Babylonian Talmud.*
[11]Maslow, *op. cit.*, p. 312.

utter folly of wickedness and the wisdom of righteousness. All things which transpire are not good, but they work in a pattern of relationship for good for those who have realized the divine purpose for life (Rom. 8:28). The Christian seldom understands the specifics or sees in detail the extent of God's working, but he knows the joy of communion, and the confidence that life is a gratifying discovery of God's purpose.

5

The Actualized Life

It is by living totally in the world that Christian personality is formed. The man who rejects serious deliberation for easy prayer makes a mockery of his faith. When he shirks responsible decision for pietistic pretense, he discredits his testimony. When he excuses inaction in the name of God's will, he denies Christ. A man can only plumb the Christian life in the world.

The Actualized Life

A psalm of David.

1. Yahweh is my shepherd, I shall not lack.
2. He causes me to lie down in green pastures. He pastures me near the waters of rest.
3. He renews my soul. He directs me in paths of righteousness for His name's sake.
4. Even when I go through the valley of death-shadow, I will not fear evil, for You are ever with me. Your rod and staff comfort me.
5. You prepare a table before me in the presence of my adversaries. You anoint my head with oil. My cup overflows.
6. Certainly, goodness and mercy shall pursue me all the days of my life, and I will dwell in the house of Yahweh for all time.

Psalm 23

A gift can be made personal only by employing it for its intended use. That which God has provided by His grace must be appropriated with reverence and diligence. (Phil. 2:12-13). There is no short cut to the making of a Christian person.

THEME

No passage more simply or beautifully expresses the vindication of life-in-God than the beloved Twenty-Third Psalm. The theme "I shall not lack" (vs. 1) could easily be repeated as a refrain throughout the psalm. The text impresses one as being deeply personal; it is a reflection upon God's faithfulness through the various aspects of life past and confidence in regard to the future. It has the nostalgic vividness of imagery recalled from an earlier shepherd's experience and applied to the deep lessons of abiding in Yahweh. Two figures, the good shepherd (vss. 1-4) and the good host (vs. 5), blend into one confident refrain (vs. 6).

The designation of Yahweh as shepherd was a familiar one (Gen. 49:24), as was that of Israel as His flock (Psa. 74:1; 100:3). It is a refreshingly idyllic picture. The shepherd leads his flock, after Eastern custom, rather than driving them before him. He knows them by name and is able to pick the individual sheep from a surging mass of seemingly identical creatures. Now and then an animal pauses to pull at especially luscious herbage or to satisfy his curiosity over an unusual phenomenon. But at the call of the recognized voice, he bounds to the shepherd's side, fondly nuzzling the outstretched hand.

Yet the Judean hillsides could be inhospitable. There was the need of seeking out grazing accommodation and fresh water, the possibility of losing the way or tumbling into a deep ravine, or of attack by wild beast or roving thief. The shepherd, experienced in the vicissitudes of pastoral life and armed to ward off the enemy, was the guarantor of good things and of safety.

The fact that there is but one shepherd (vs. 1) does not mean that his sheep are identical. There is always the danger of what Erich Fromm calls "being an automaton among automata"—that is of conforming to what others expect of you. The error is the more serious for being perpetrated in God's name. Christians should be the most different people imaginable, not simply from non-Christians, but from each other. This differentiation of personality around the reality of authentic living is the goal of the actualized life. It cannot be reproduced by imitation; it is produced only by the experience of fellowship through the tensions of spiritual growth.

Carl Jung has made a major contribution to our understanding of individuation, the means by which selfhood may be achieved. He explains: "It is a relatively rare occurrence, which is experienced only by those who have gone through the wearisome but, if the unconscious is to be integrated, indispensable business of coming to terms with the unconscious components of the personality."[1] Contrary to much popular expectation, Christianity offers no *simple* solution to man's problems or to the integration of his personality; it does promise the abiding presence of Christ in the resolution of difficulties and toward the development of Christian character. There is no offer of ease, but the promise of grace for the experience.

The psalmist steers between the presumption of total control over either the exigencies of life or his personal responses, and despair concerning the external and internal forces which resist progress. He is not like the neurotic who "calls for a goal of absolute, godlike power, [and] with his customary dogmatism, must attain absolute success or nothing at all."[2] He knows that life consists of imperfectly realizing the total sufficiency of God. He can rejoice in the availability of grace and grow through the demands which life places upon it.

PAUSE BY THE WAY

Life is made up of a variety of experiences. Some of these the psalmist pictures in a series of pastoral episodes: the watering of the flock, the shepherd's guidance over the uncharted paths, and

[1]Carl Jung, "Patterns of Behavior and Archetypes," *Theories of Personality*, Lindzey and Hall, eds., p. 71.
[2]Abraham and Edith Luchins, *Rigidity of Behavior*, p. 21.

protection through the dangerous ravines. In each of these instances the psalmist finds his Lord sufficient.

When the sun beats down fiercely from overhead, the shepherd leads his flock to cool meadows (vs. 2). *Nahul* is a distinctively pastoral word, implying gentle leading. The shepherd is solicitous in his concern. Waiting for the flock is tender growth to soothe the warm bodies, and waters by which they rest. It is a time for relaxing and refreshing. The shepherd draws water to quench the thirst, and allows the flock to relax upon the soft green growth.

Man needs time to contemplate, restore his energies, and gain perspective. He must find occasions to move out of the torrid pace of life. In the quietness his anxious thoughts are tempered and his obsessive drives are stilled. He draws upon the resources of God, and is refreshed in spirit. Ahead are difficult testings, but this is the time to prepare for them rather than to pursue their resolution. The pause will sustain the rugged climb.

LIGHT ON THE SECULAR

Again the shepherd's voice is heard (vs. 3b). It is time to pass on. He goes before. The sheep leave behind the pleasant pastures which were not meant for continuous repose. As Jung observes: "Individuation does not shut one out from the world, but gathers the world to oneself."[3]

It is by living totally in the world that Christian personality is formed. The man who rejects serious deliberation for easy prayer makes a mockery of his faith. When he shirks responsible decision for pietistic pretense, he discredits his testimony. When he excuses inaction in the name of God's will, he denies Christ. A man can only plumb the Christian life in the world. It involves "taking life in one's stride, with all its duties and problems, its successes and failures, its experiences and helplessness. It is in such a life that we throw ourselves utterly into the arms of God and participate in his sufferings in the world and watch with Christ in Gethsemane. That is faith, that is *metanoia*, and that is what makes a man a Christian."[4]

[3]Jung, *op. cit.*, p. 72.
[4]Dietrich Bonhoeffer, *Letters and Papers from Prison*, p. 125.

The intensity of such participation explains the need of renewal. We can shield ourselves against other persons by manipulating them as things, but true interpersonal involvement is demanding. Such was the Lord's experience (John 4:6), and so will be that of His disciples.

Homeostasis, a tensionless state, is not the personal ideal to covet. What man requires is "the striving and struggling for some goal worthy of him. What he needs is not the discharge of tension at any cost, but the call of a potential meaning waiting to be fulfilled by him."[5] Each step forward requires leaving behind something familiar and satisfying, and involves something unknown and threatening. It demands more and more of leaving the world of egocentricity, and entering into the orbits of other persons. It is an experience of paradoxical gain and loss (Matt. 10:39).

As the Christian throws himself wholly into the world, he casts himself fully on God. There is the promise of guidance coupled with renewal (vs. 3). Christianity is a distinctive involvement which invites our more detailed investigation.

The Christian Perspective

Oliver Barclay suggests that the Christian norm for guidance is "sound judgment based on a truly Christian sense of values."[6] He adds that this wisdom is not identical with common sense, but is rather man's judgment elevated by revelation. Scripture is explicit: "You shall therefore keep my statutes and my ordinances, by doing of which a man shall live. I am Yahweh" (Lev. 18:5); and "I have laid up Thy word in my heart, that I might not sin against You" (Psa. 119:11).

Rabbinic commentary is quite helpful at this point. For instance, it reflects that the study of the Torah by the heathen makes him as good as the High Priest. Devotion to the Torah is not an excuse from but occasion for piety. As "Resh Lakish said: 'The commandment of the Lord is pure' [Psa. 19:9]. If one's intent is pure, the Torah for him becomes a life-giving medicine, purifying him to life. But if one's intent is not pure, it becomes a

[5]Frankl, op. cit., p. 107.
[6]Oliver Barclay, Guidance: Some Biblical Principles, p. 9.

death-giving drug, purifying him to death."[7] The word is to be handled with reverential devotion and enthusiastic obedience: "Hasten to perform the slightest commandment, and flee from sin; for the performance of one commandment leads to another an one transgression leads to another. The reward of a commandment is another to be fulfilled, and the reward of one transgression is another."[8]

The Christian is involved in life's struggle along with others who may or may not share his faith. He is perhaps least sensitive to the difference caused by his allegiance to Holy Writ. His peculiarity is not one of his own making or maintained by his determination, but is the result of God's grace. Guidance is a natural development of the life in communion with the Word—Christ; devoutly immersed in the word—Scripture.

The growing Christian will experience the frustration of un-sheltered living (Job 1:10-12). His life can border on the line of despair, so intense may stress become, for his faith makes him more rather than less human. In the depth of living he finds the true extent of God's grace, and the means which mold him into the image of Christ. There he realizes the resources of God for himself, and makes them available to his fellows. He does not come empty-handed to the human struggle.

Authentic Reality

The believer has not only the advantage of perspective, but the personal reality of grace (II Cor. 3:3). We dare not conclude that he per se knows more than other men or has some special insight into the course of action which should be taken. He does not become as a result of his conversion an expert on labor relations, population explosion, or civil rights. What he does bring to these and other critical areas is the concern for righteousness, the honor of God's name (vs. 3). His prayer is for God's will to be done, and the promise he claims is to be led into paths of righteousness. He does not play God, but prays to Him.

The Christian can forgive because he has been forgiven. He

[7] *Yoma*, 72b, quoted in *Judaism*, A. Hertzberg, ed., p. 76.
[8] *Mishnah Avot*, 4:2, quoted in *ibid.*, pp. 183-4.

can love because he has been loved. Grace received can be mediated.

Some years ago I became acquainted wtih a young man of most desolate character. He was abhorred by his associates, who singled him out for extreme mental cruelty and even physical brutality. He had no home and no friends and was fed on a constant diet of hate. Some time passed. It was reported to me that this man had been converted to Christ, and subsequent observation seemed to confirm it. There was a lack of pretension, and a quiet confidence that seemed now to commend him to his peers, a winsomeness and concern about him which exuded the reality he had found in Christ. A dynamic of love had replaced that of hate. His life illustrates better than words the authentic reality which the Christian brings to the routine of existence.

We have seen that God's preferred classroom for building Christian character is the world rather than the monastery. The Christian is in the world, but not of it. He brings a perspective sharpened in Scripture and a continuing experience of grace. Perfection always escapes him. He is in the process of proving the sufficiency of God, and the process (rather than the goal set before him) is God's witness to men.

EVEN THERE

The "death-shadow" (vs. 4) traditionally has been interpreted as a reference to the passing of life; as such, the verse has been of the greatest comfort to those going through this experience. The best that can be said for the idea is that it is an application of the text. "Death-shade is a strong poetical expression for the profoundest darkness."[9] The Judean hill country is broken up by narrow and precipitous fissures, shrouded in forboding darkness, abounding with caves concealing robbers and wild beasts. Such is the nature of the danger awaiting the flock. Something of the idea of death-shadow is seen in the use of the word in reference to Hades (Job 10:21), uninhabited desert (Jer. 2:6), and mine shaft (Job 28:3).

---

[9]John Calvin, *Commentary on the Book of Psalms*, I, p. 196.

Even in the death-shadow the psalmist will not fear. More threatening than finding the right paths of the hills are the deep, forbidding ravines. Though the psalmist will not be without fear, he will surmount it with confidence in the shepherd. His eyes shift from the terrifying darkness to the dim outline of the staff. It is likely that the psalmist had only one implement in mind, but one with a double use: the rod to protect and the staff to guide. By calling it a staff, the psalmist may imply that the shepherd leans upon it as he carefully watches the sheep, or uses it to extricate them from a precarious situation. The tendency to be afraid or agitated over the death-shadow and any imaginative speculation is checked by the protector's presence. The symbol of his office dispels the gloom.

The passage describes God's working with His people in the most extreme and threatening of life's experiences. The nature of the experience which terrifies differs from person to person. An Army buddy of mine was so frightened at the thought of snakes that the turning of a twig underfoot could and sometimes did cause him to dash for "safety" yards away from the object. His death-shade was a snake pit. Man wants to think that when he trusts, he will not fear; but the more realistic confession is: "When I am afraid, I put my trust in You" (Psa. 56:3). Courage is born when man faces fear in a cause.

There is a sense in which the extremity is welcomed, not for the terror involved, but for the opportunity it holds for growth and witness. The Christian does not ask for such a testing, but he is content to believe that if he is called upon to go through it, he will not be alone.

GOOD TIMES

Life is not for most an unbroken chain of mishaps or near-tragedies. There are the good times. Our metaphors now shift from the flock to that of the guest-right (vs. 5). It was considered a sacred duty to extend protection and hospitality (Gen. 19:1-11; Judg. 19:22-25). A more recent incident illustrates the same attitude. A missionary was handed a piece of mutton, accompanied by his host's explanation: "By that act I have pledged you every drop of my blood, that while you are in my territory no evil shall come to you. For that space of time we are brothers."[10]

While the image of the overflowing cup is meant to reinforce the idea of the host's liberality, anointing with oil symbolizes the happiness of the occasion (Psa. 45:7; 104:15). Such exhilarating times are part of Christian experience. These are appropriate occasions for reflecting on God's faithfulness.

The two metaphors merge in retrospect (vs. 6). The psalmist looks back, as if expecting to see the enemy in pursuit. Instead, he sees only the personification of goodness and mercy acting as rear guard. As often as he turns about, they stand watchful. The same is true of the hospitality extended to him. He continues to enjoy the protection, bounty, and fellowship of the home. The favor which he experiences is so great that he regards all else as unworthy to be considered even as an exception. As pain is soon forgotten, the blessing of God bathes the wounds and recalls the good learned through leaner times.

We have seen how God plans to build Christian character through the varied aspects of life. While the experience of each person differs from the experience of others, and from time to time alters radically from what he has experienced in the past, the faithfulness of God remains the same (Heb. 13:8). There is no lack for the Christian who is in the process of actualizing his life, no want of sustaining grace.

THE GOOD SHEPHERD

When Jesus called Himself "the good shepherd," he was not only calling to mind the familiar imagery of the psalmist, but He was also clearly identifying Himself with Yahweh by using the formula: "I am" (cf. Job 8:58). Ethelbert Stauffer succinctly summarizes the significance of the testimony: "He was in all deliberation using the Old Testament and liturgical formula of God's self-revelation. He wished to convey that in his life the historical epiphany of God was taking place."[11] The radical

---

[11] Ethelbert Stauffer, *Jesus and His Story*, p. 193.
[10] H. Clay Trumbull, *Studies in Oriental Social Life*, p. 110.

nature of His claim was attested by the miraculous nature of His acts and the still more astounding character of His person.

The Good Shepherd discourse is introduced by the words "Truly, truly" (John 10:1). This phrase appears never to be used to introduce a new situation. This fact along with a consideration of the content of the passage, gives us sufficient reason to treat the discourse in connection with the earlier claims of Christ, and the subsequent excommunication of one who embraced His way.

The religious leaders in Jerusalem were concerned because Christ had healed a blind beggar on the Sabbath. Some protested: "This man is not from God, for he does not keep the Sabbath"; others wondered, "How can a man who is a sinner do such a sign?" (John 9:16). They turned on the beggar, first interrogating and then dismissing him from the synagogue. Christ responded to their hostility in the form of a parable (John 10).

Religion professes to deal with divinity. The religious leader approaches God on behalf of his constituency, and presumes to speak for God to man. The temptation is for the leader to conclude that he is not only a guide of men, but also a manipulator of the holy. He believes that through the prescribed rites, he has contained the Almighty and enslaved Him to a system. God then becomes the means of sanctioning man's subjection of his fellow. This tendency is evident in the legalistic attitude expressed here by the Pharisees toward the Sabbath, in their insensitive feeling for the man restored to sight and their subsequent excommunication of him which carried not only religious but social and economic sanctions.

The good shepherd, by contrast, does not treat man as a thing to be manipulated but as a person to be aided (John 10:3). He does not prey on the sheep (vs. 10), but gives himself to them (vs. 15). He does not take flight as those who are afraid of the excommunication ban (vs. 13), but lays down his life for the sheep (vs. 18). Jesus identifies Himself as that Good Shepherd (vs. 11).

The previously blind man was faced with a decision between the demand of religion and the call of Christ. The former attempted to bribe him into the religious sanctuary, while the latter invited him into human struggle. He had to decide between being immobilized by sanction, or striving for actualization. It was not an easy decision; and it was one which he would have to face time and again.

At the heart of the religious escape from life is indolence, the unwillingness to bear the pain of responsible decision. "Religious people speak of God when human perception is (often just from laziness) at an end, or human resources fail."[12] God becomes the convenient excuse for lack of preparation or laziness in pursuit of the task, and carelessness in reappraisal. The religious person thus answers every question with the blanket response: "God wanted it this way." He supposes that guidance dehumanizes man, rather than lifting human capabilities to new potential.

The religious person fails to understand that what he presumes to be God's voice is more likely that of his parents, his society, and/or his interest. His mistake is not only that he fails to discern God's word, but perpetuates his error on posterity.

Clues to the existence of the religious mentality are a summary treatment of others, and the effort to coerce faith. Christ stood in sharpest contrast to these characteristics. He associated with the outcasts of society. He accepted persons as He found them, and dismissed them only as they were unwilling to look with similar honesty to themselves (John 9:41).

Christ knew best the dire consequences of rejection of the gospel, but never took advantage of circumstances or applied inordinate pressure to gain a following. His treatment of the restored man is a commentary on tenderness with the personality of another (John 9:7, 30-39).

The road to the actualized life also has two clues: openness to all, and openness with every man. The term "fullness" (plērōma) best describes the universal availability of the growing Christian (John 10:10). Paul uses it to describe the gathering of the Gentiles (Rom. 11:25). "This 'incoming' can and shall take place only because Christ is already the plērōma himself, the totality of the Word of God made flesh; for from him there flows the whole fulness of divine grace and truth."[13] The life cannot be expected

---

[12]Bonhoeffer, Letters and Papers from Prison, p. 93.
[13]George A. F. Knight (ed.), Jews and Christians: Preparation for Dialogue, p. 49.

to mature in Christ so long as the disciple restricts from his consideration those who are part of his Lord's concern.

The disciple must enlarge his horizons not only to embrace all but to accept each man as he finds him. It is possible to live with another person in close proximity over an extended period without ever seeing him as he is. The person we know is actually only the figment of our imagination. Christ did not make men over in order to accept them, but accepted them in order to make them over. The world of self-actualization is an interpersonal society where the dynamic of Christian love is being realized.

TERMINATION

It is not surprising that the Christian faith should have first been described as "the way" (Acts 19:9, 23; 24:14). God's gift does not come neatly packaged; it is mediated through the experiences of life. Each step of faith is calculated to reap spiritual benefit. The actualized life does not come vicariously from but through Christ. It is forged in life's crucible.

We have traced the detail of life from the restorative retirement, over the rocky path of daily routine, through both the threatening experience and the good time when evil seems held at bay. Most will recognize such varied aspects of their lives, although these overlap and crowd in upon each other. In the variation of life's circumstances the Christian finds God's sufficiency and the potential to cope with life's demands. Grace does not come in advance, as if to allow us to squander it upon ourselves; but it is there when it is needed. There remains the abiding confidence that "I shall not want." In the words of Aaron Wolfe and James M. Gray:

> Complete in Thee—each want supplied,
> And no good thing to me denied;
> Since Thou my portion, Lord, will be,
> I ask no more, complete in Thee.

Christ still looks upon the multitude with compassion (Matt. 9:36). They are described as flayed (skullō), skinned by friction with the hard realities of life, and cast down or away *(hriptō)*, discarded like an old coat by society. The Master's concern is translated into the ministry of His people. The Christian must turn his back on every pressure to turn him into an automaton, and most emphatically from anything which smacks of religious escapism. The gift of authentic life is meant to be actualized in the world of interpersonal relationships and service.

6

Crucible of Pain

Pain is real, and the man-less-pain is a man-less-human- | *oui pain*
ity. To live is to suffer. There is no other world; only
the one created in man's imagination conforms to his
advantage. To accept one's humanity is to accept this
life and the pain that attends it.

Crucible of Pain

To the choir director concerning the hind of the morning.
A psalm of David.

1. My God, my God, why have You forsaken me? Why are You far from helping me, from the groaning of my words?
2. My God, I cry by day, but You answer not, and at night there is no repose for me.
3. Yet You are holy, You Who are enthroned upon the praises of Israel.
4. Our fathers trusted in You; they trusted and You delivered them.
5. They cried unto You and were delivered. They trusted in You and were not ashamed.
6. But I (am) a worm and not a man, a reproach of man and despised by the people.
7. All those that see me mock at me. They open the lip. They wag the head, (saying):
8. "He commits his way to Yahweh; let Him deliver him. Let Him rescue him, for He delights in him."
9. Yet You are He that took me from the womb. You caused me to trust upon my mother's breast.
10. Upon You was I cast from my birth. You (are) my God from my mother's womb.
11. Be not far from me, for trouble is near and there is none to help.
12. Many bulls have surrounded me, (those) mighty of Bashan have encompassed me.
13. They open their mouth at me, as a ravening and roaring lion.
14. I am poured out like water, and my bones are dislocated. My heart is like wax. It is melted in my innermost part.
15. My strength has dried like a potsherd, my tongue sticks to my jaws, and You lay me in the dust of death.

away my keeper to pull me bone by bone

16. For dogs have surrounded me. The company of the wicked have enclosed me, like a lion at my hands and feet.
17. I can count all my bones. They look and rejoice over me.
18. They divide my garments among them, and cast lots for my garments.
19. But You, Yahweh, be not far from me; my Strength, hasten to help me.
20. Deliver my soul from the sword, my life from the might of the dog.
21. Save me from the mouth of the lion, and from the horns of the wild oxen. Answer me!
22. I will declare Your name to my brothers. In the midst of the congregation I will praise You.
23. You that fear Yahweh, praise Him. All the seed of Jacob, glorify Him; and fear Him, all the seed of Israel.
24. For He neither despised nor abhorred the oppression of the afflicted, nor hid His face from them, but when they cried unto Him, He heard.
25. I shall praise You in the great congregation. I will pay my vows before those who fear Him.
26. The afflicted will eat and be satisfied. Those who seek Him shall praise Yahweh. May your heart live for ever.
27. All the ends of the earth shall remember and turn to Yahweh, and all the families of the nations shall worship before You.
28. For the kingdom (is) Yahweh's, and He (is) the ruler over the nations.
29. All the prosperous of the earth shall eat and worship, and all those who are abased shall bow before Him.
30. An offspring shall serve Him. It shall be told of the Lord for a generation.
31. They shall come and declare His righteousness to a people to be born that He has done it. PSALM 22

There is likely no more pressing subject than the meaning of pain. Man cannot escape suffering, but the attitude which he takes toward it may be altered. His response makes the difference between emotional health and illness and may demonstrate, if not an insight into the purpose of pain, at least an ability to handle it constructively.

PROBLEM

The context of the psalmist's question is as significant as the content, and his assumptions about suffering are as important as his query concerning why he was subjected to it. One reason the question of pain goes unanswered is that it is asked in a framework where no adequate solution is possible. Consequently, we need to see the perspective from which the psalmist views the issue.

The Reality of Pain

Earlier we noted that the Scripture makes the realistic assumption that the world has objective reality. There is nothing illusory about pain, whether it comes from a physical wound or from mental anguish. Its resolution inevitably begins with the recognition of its inescapable presence.

The significance of the psalmist's position can best be seen by comparing it with a rather diametrically opposed solution, the teaching of Gautama, the alleged founder of Buddhism. Reported to have died in 545 B.C., Gautama left behind his discovery of the meaning of life, summarized in the Four Noble Truths:

1. *Life is suffering.* Perhaps the term "unhappiness" or "frustration" would be preferable to "suffering." Gautama observed that finite existence consisted of sickness, old age, death, and the sadness experienced when loved ones are stricken. These frustrations (*dukha*) constitute the problem of life.

2. *Suffering is caused by desire.* Frustration is caused by grasping (*trishna*), asking from life what it cannot give us. It is not simply asking more, but asking at all that perpetuates the self and the frustration which attends it. Man interferes with nature in such a way that he is compelled to continue interfering, and the resolution of each problem creates still other problems.

3. *Desire may be destroyed.* The ending of desire is called *nirvana,* a release or liberation. *Nirvana* defies precise definition, for the very effort at definition is grasping, and release comes when clutching at life has come to an end.

4. *The means of elimination is the Eightfold Path.* In summary, the Eightfold Path concerns apprehension and application. Man sees the folly of grasping after the distinction between "I" and "not I," and rises above the phenomenal world through *dhyana* (a word best left untranslated, for such words as meditation and absorption are misleading). Gautama took his stance under the Bodhi tree until he knew such destruction was possible, and others have confirmed his discovery.

The resolution of suffering offered by Gautama is not unique to Buddhism. It consists of rejecting the essential reality of the empirical world in so far as meaning is concerned, and thus eliminating the issue of pain. Gautama consoled a grieving widow who had lost her only son with the observation that she who has many children for whom to care has much suffering, but she who has none has least.

Against such a conceptual backdrop, the psalmist's belief stands out in bold relief. The resolution of pain consists not in escaping but in engagement, not in ignoring but in heeding the senses, not in rejecting but in entertaining the question which pain raises. Pain is real, and the man-less-pain is a man-less-humanity. To live is to suffer. There is no other world; only the one created in man's imagination conforms to his advantage. To accept one's humanity is to accept *this* life and the pain that attends it.

Quest of Faith

A common misconception is that faith asks no questions, presumably because it holds all the needed answers. Such is not the case. Sound faith aids a person in asking *profitable* questions. The psalmist's query springs from belief rather than unbelief. It addresses God in the time of trouble rather than forsaking Him in order to despair.

Faith is as critical to the solution of the problem of pain as admitting the pressing reality of suffering itself. The effort of

Karl Marx is a negative illustration in point. Marx was a nine-teenth-century social reformer who recognized something of the injustice of his time and the affliction which accompanied it. He was concerned with human suffering, but he understood it primarily as a social phenomenon. That is, he saw man essentially as class rather than as person. Marx held out for the exploited working man a utopia where he would experience "from each according to his ability, to each according to his need."

The road of faith was blocked to Marx by the apparent indifference of the institutionalized Church. He charged that religion was the opiate of the people, the means of anesthetizing man against social struggle. Conversely, he erred in at least two critical points: failing to take the individual dimension of suffering seriously, and rejecting faith as a workable perspective for resolving the problem.

It is unrealistic to suppose that one can substitute concern over class struggle for the needs of the individual. A cause which indefinitely postpones personal considerations seems destined to perpetuate itself by force. The Marxist dogma has proved to be its own opiate to the problem of personal pain. It ignores the issue which faith has the courage to raise. Every man is important, not simply as a producer or for his value to society, but because he is a noble creature of God. Every issue which troubles him cries for consideration. The fact of suffering demands attention, and the faith of the sufferer comes to his assistance.

Confidence in a Moral Universe

Western man has little problem with the reality of pain, nor does he entertain lightly the role of faith; it is the affirmation of a moral universe which seems questionable. The psalmist's confidence that God is working redemptively with man seems shattered by the bewildering and degenerate aspects of contemporary civilization. God may exist, but we do not understand how He works, least of all in human suffering.

Our problem is seeing the unity of purpose in the diversity of events. The issue is anything but new. The effort to find national destiny in the midst of the changing fortunes of war is admirably reflected in Homer's Olympian gods. In a classic passage he describes the council of the gods over the military affairs of man. Zeus passes judgment on the request to join in the struggle:

> For which call'd ye; true, they needs must die,
> But still they claim my care; yet here will I
> Upon Olympus' lofty ridge remain,
> And view, serene, the combat: you, the rest,
> Go, as you let, to Trojans or to Greeks,
> And at your pleasure either party aid.[1]

So the gods joined men in mortal combat.

The Greek solution was to project the imperfection of humanity and the accidents of life on the gods. The meaning of suffering might not be understood as such, but no doubt the answer had to do with the caprice of the gods who involved themselves in the affairs of men. But the resolution lacked rectitude; the gods were characterized by human failings.

Contemporary handling of the problem is hardly more sophisticated. Suffering is recognized as being an aspect of authentic living—inexplicable, mysterious, but somehow necessary. The issue is demanding, but no solution seems within sight.

The psalmist, however, profers the context of God's moral purpose, a place where faith can ask the important question, "Why?"

PLIGHT

The believer is not free from the fact or immune from the stress of suffering. He brings to the situation faith both in God and in His purpose being realized, a faith which can question the seeming disparity between the ideal and the present incident. He has a faith of such realistic dimension that it can question God. Similarly, Rabbi Livi quotes the protest (vs. 1) for Queen Esther, and adds: "Dost thou perchance punish the inadvert offense like the presumptuous one, or one done under compulsion like one done willingly?"[2]

---

[1] *Iliad*, XIX, 25-30. Translated by Richmond Lattimore. Copyright 1951 by the University of Chicago.
[2] *Megillah*, 15b. *The Babylonian Talmud.*

The question is demanded because of the tension between faith and fulfillment in the suffering role. Were it not for faith, there would be no one to turn to. The atheist may complain, but only the believer can protest. On the other hand, if it were not for the reality of pain, no question would be necessary. The resulting tension between faith and fulfillment, far from being ill advised, may provide the key to resolution.

Before proceeding further, we must clarify the nature of faith and fulfillment. Faith is in God's good intention toward man (vss. 5,9). God is holy, *qadash* meaning to be separate or set apart (vs. 3). As applied to the Almighty, it suggests His transcendence of being and attribute. As related to His dealing with man, God's unswerving justice and resolute promise are implied.

The story is told of four traveling rabbis who had heard the tumult of the city of Rome in the distance. Three wept but the fourth laughed. When the three were asked why they wept, they replied: "These heathen, who worship and burn incense to idols, live here in peace and security, while our Temple, the footstool at the Throne of God, is destroyed by fire. How should we not weep?" The fourth, Rabbi Akiva, answered: "That is why I laugh. If this is the lot of those who transgress His will, how much more glorious shall be the lot of those who perform His will."[3]

It may be pointed out that the confidence of Rabbi Akiva, no less than that of the psalmist, has had impressive justification in the history of God's dealing with man. The psalmist recalls that the fathers trusted and were delivered (vs. 4). The testing of the psalmist and the loss of the Temple caused concern for but were not a lack of God's providential continuity. Faith is not sight, but it is not absurd. Reason moves in the same direction, but lacks the finality of faith. It cannot prove conclusively what faith can respectfully entertain. For the psalmist, God's writing can be seen in human events, but at points its meaning becomes illegible.

What then is the meaning of life fulfillment in suffering? It is living life as we find it, without demanding exceptions or prefer-

---

[3]*Makkot*, 24b. Quoted in Hertzberg, ed., *Judaism*, p. 201.

ential treatment. It is keeping our sensitivity awake to all that life, and life in Christ, is to mean. A provocative speculation on Christ's refusal to take the stupefying drink offered at the crucifixion, contrasts His openness to man's defense: "By deadening pain, by mental chloroform, by drugging our spirits, we keep our lives from being exposed to costly sympathy. But we also keep them from being exposed to the spirit of God."[4]

We shield ourselves from life by ignoring the report or refusing to view the sordidness and suffering of the world. We cut ourselves off from people, conceiving them as objects rather than subjects. We reject even our own suffering by postponing consideration or by a flight into unreality. In so doing, we divorce ourselves not only from life but from the God of the living.

PAIN

Having weighed the meaning of faith and fulfillment, we may look at the experience of suffering *per se*. The psalmist characterizes it as forsakenness (vs. 1) and futility (vss. 11-18).

Forsakenness

To be forsaken is no longer to experience the company and/or support of the one in whom confidence is placed. Forsakenness is a subjective conclusion, based at least in part on an objective indication. It may express not so much a person's true and abiding conviction as the intensity of the torment through which he is going. It is here we likely find the clue to the psalmist's experience.

One cannot experience the answer to life until he feels the question. All the consideration prior to the question is academic, ivory-tower, unincarnated. The cry of the psalmist is not a reasoned reflection but the moan of a pain-ridden man. The use of *Eli* as an appeal to God perhaps suggests in its brevity, the gasp of agony. Or, because of its context, it may suggest the One who is in a position to be of help (vs. 1).

---

[4]Halford C. Luccock, *The Interpreter's Bible*, VII, p. 902.

The answer does not come easily, and it cannot be learned by rote. The idea of belief has to be forged into the experience of trust. The poet persists (vs. 2), realizing that anything less is defeat.

Pain is intensified by disregard. The psalmist is mocked by those who pass by (vss. 6-8). They gesture rudely and speak of him with contempt. Their conclusion is that he is "no man" (vs. 6). The Rabbinic commentary on this verse is pointed: "Therefore a single man was first created in the world, to teach that if any man causes a single soul to perish, Scripture considers him as though he had caused an entire world to perish; and if any man saves a single soul, Scripture considers him as though he had saved an entire world."[5]

Is there anything more difficult than not to be accepted as a fellow human? I have a sensitive friend living out the last years of his life in a convalescent home where the attendants perform the least responsibilities begrudgingly and without feeling. Viktor Frankl had to watch his valuable manuscript discarded by a calloused concentration camp guard. By the depersonalization of hostility a person is transformed into a thing, a *he* to an *it*. The *man* Jesus died to the screaming multitude before ever He reached Golgotha. The words of imprecation and acts of violence eclipsed the nature of His humanity.

Futility

The intensity of pain crowds out even the torment of man's cruelty. The tempo of the psalm picks up quickly: "my trouble is near" (vs. 11), "like a lion at my hands and feet" (vs. 16), and "hasten to help me" (vs. 19). The language is exceedingly vivid. Lions crouch to spring upon and devour him (vs. 13). He is like water dissipated upon the ground, his bones out of joint, his inner being melted into wax (vs. 14). He is as parched as a potsherd, as a tongue stuck to the roof of the mouth, and as a man laid in the dust of death (vs. 15). Wild dogs surround him and lions are at his limbs. His flesh is so wasted away that his bones can be numbered (vs. 17). The feelings of being forsaken and rejected are

---

[5]*Sanhedrin*, 4:5. *The Babylonian Talmud.*

swept away by utter helplessness. He is powerless to cope with the critical threat to his existence.

Suffering defies explanation. Analysis and imagery still fall short of the experience, but the one who has known severe pain will have no difficulty in identifying the emotion which has been expressed. The more critical question concerns the attitude taken toward one's suffering. In this, as in other matters, the Christian will desire the mental attitude of Christ (Phil. 2:5).

Fellowship

Christ entered into human suffering. He quoted the words of the psalmist in terms of His own experience on the cross (Matt. 27:46; Mark 15:34). While it is true that He suffered *for* man, our concern here is that He also suffered *with* man. That is, what does the fellowship of suffering imply?

Probably more important than the manner in which Christ entertained his ordeal is the fact of His suffering *per se*. Man is never called upon to undergo a more severe testing than that which Christ, in love, undertook. No word of encouragement from the sidelines could approach what this means to the suffering saint. That He has become one with us in pain is more important than the finer theoretical points to be deduced. There is a bond of divine-human suffering into which the believer enters. There is an intimacy forged in pain.

Rabbi Mendel was once approached by a man agonizing over the death of his wife in childbirth, leaving him with the infant child and six other small children. The Rabbi listened respectfully with eyes lowered. After a moment of meditation, he raised his head, looking deeply into the eyes of his questioner, and speaking earnestly: "I am not equal to the task of consoling you after such cruel suffering. Only the true Master of mercy is equal to that. Turn to Him."[6] If the fellowship of men in suffering consoles, how much more the fellowship with the Lord in pain?

What more may be said of the manner in which one suffers? The psalmist entertains the possibility that God's purpose may be furthered in his death (vs. 15). Job, the man who personifies suf-

---

[6]Arthur Hertzberg, *Judaism*, p. 203.

fering, could attest: "Though He slay me, yet will I trust Him" (Job 3:15a). Christ could pray for God's will, recognizing that this could incorporate the cross (Luke 22:42). The man who can accept the worst possible alternative in faith is the man who is freed from its terror. Death is far from the worst thing to the believer's imagination. Prolonged illness, the loss of physical and mental capacities, and the burden placed on loved ones are far more threatening possibilities. But to the man who can face even these alternatives in the fellowship of divine suffering, there is no fear to stalk him.

"But You" (vs. 19) is emphatic. The psalmist contrasts God with the persecutors, and prays for deliverance (vs. 20). Life is precious and to be valued. The believer does not seek to throw his life away any more than he tries to save it at the cost of disobedience to God's will. He maintains a healthy, positive attitude toward living. The Christian dies hard but courageously and confidently. More important than the outcome is the divine fellowship attributed to the moment. Yahweh is there in the midst of the testing; He is there in the communion of fellowship.

Some years ago a provocative interchange was reported to me. A devout woman was taken quite ill, and several of her friends came to visit her. It is often difficult to know how to engage a suffering person in appropriate conversation, so after a painful silence one of the visitors blurted out: "I suppose that you are much in prayer that health will quickly return." The woman answered out of a life which had learned the secret of gracious perseverance: "I am praying, but for the purpose that the illness not pass until I have learned all the lessons God intends for me." The reality of God's presence is ministered in many ways, but seldom more effectively than in pain.

We have seen the experience of suffering within its larger context of human existence. There is reason to believe that man suffers disproportionately to that experienced by other created life. His pain takes the form of feeling forsaken, of being bypassed by life itself, cursed by mankind. An oppressive futility settles upon Him so that words of explanation fail. The believer is not immune from this event or experience, but he does derive consolation from the fellowship of divine suffering. He knows not what the hour will bring, but he has the confidence that the Lord will in any case sustain him.

PURPOSE

It may seem presumptive even to consider trying to understand the purpose of pain. The explanation given here will hardly exhaust the possibilities, and may not even provide the best direction in which to look. However, even a partial answer is better than ignoring the issue.

We may assume that the primary significance of life is not avoiding pain at all cost, as Frankl concludes: "man's main concern is not to gain pleasure or to avoid pain but rather to see a meaning in his life. That is why man is even ready to suffer, on the condition, to be sure, that his suffering has a meaning."[7] If the problem of pain is to be realistically treated, it must be handled within a larger framework. Pain is not bad when it warns us of a serious injury and is not evil if it provides a service to man in his situation.

The World

Creation is not a self-sustaining entity. The foundations of the universe are laid by God, and as a garment it will some day be folded up (Heb. 1:11-12). All things are said to consist or hold together in Christ (Col. 1:16-17). In the light of the context of Paul's statement in Colossians, it seems that God's sustaining purpose is redemptive in nature. Scores of verses may be summoned to support this thesis. Life provides a variety of significance, but the meaning is restoration of man in Christ.

Pain is best understood against the backdrop of redemptive need and purpose. It is a fact that "pain insists upon being attended to. God whispers to us in our pleasures, speaks to us in our conscience, but shouts in our pains: it is His megaphone to rouse a deaf world."[8] Man is in spiritual need. Pain may be the urgent warning which otherwise would go unheeded.

---

[7]Frankl, *op. cit.*, p. 115.
[8]C. S. Lewis, *The Problem of Pain*, p. 93.

The world is pictured not only as the scene of God's redemptive activity but as an arena of war (Eph. 6:10-17). There are casualties in any conflict. While there are no noncombatants in the great spiritual struggle, those who are relatively inoffensive still must suffer as a result. Who is to say that this is not the best of all possible situations, granting the depravity which spoils the land and the conflict raging as a result? Can man judge God in this matter (Job 42:3)? Does the man who suffers from the destruction understand the strategy of the conflict? There will always be the question raised by the psalmist (vs. 1), repeated by Christ, and asked again here. The answer comes in general terms, but the specific application awaits the experience, the opportunity of realizing God's sustaining grace and loving concern in a pain-filled world from which He would not even spare Himself.

Witness

The believer in a qualified sense becomes part of God's redemptive means of reconciling man. The Christian is a witness (Acts 2:32, 22:15, 26:16). A casual perusal of the context of these and other New Testament references to testimony suggests a primary concern with the resurrection of Christ. The witness points backward in terms of the life which dies in Christ, and onward in the victory experience. This dual testimonial may be seen in the rationale of suffering.

The vast majority of human affliction is due to the wickedness of man toward his fellow. The believer, in bearing his torment with forgiveness, mirrors man's depravity to him. Similarly, he repudiates that manner of life which previously had characterized him. So long as faith produces saints, and the world makes of them martyrs, there is an abiding judgment against fallen man. In the suffering which is produced we catch a glimpse of our evil intent.

Witness is not only to fault but to faith, to the fruition of grace in the believer's experience. A godly person was dying of a painful and prolonged illness. Two visitors were struck by the radical change which they saw in his emaciated body and drawn face. They talked with him briefly and excused themselves for not staying longer. Upon leaving the hospital room, one remarked:

"How can you believe in God after seeing such suffering as that?" The other replied: "How can one fail to believe in the presence of such faith as that?" One was impressed by the fact that the person was nearing the grave, but the other in that he had left the grave with Christ.

The Way

It has already been implied that the believer should engage suffering with an openness, a lack of restraint. Pain is intensified by involuntary reactions to its presence. It is man's attitude toward suffering which makes it such a monstrous terror. Faith is the power of *realistic* thinking, confidence placed in a Christ who came into a flesh-and-blood world and suffered with an intensity no man has felt. The way of suffering is not one of life denial, but of acceptance and, with Christ's consolation and strength, of triumph.

Openness is coupled with resolution and determination is based upon conviction. Suffering is the time to call upon the provisions of the past, to recall God's faithfulness: "It is better to take refuge in Yahweh than to put confidence in princes" (Psa. 118:8, 9). Cohen observes of the psalmist that "the mocking words of his persecutors have the effect of deepening his consciousness of what God had been to him since his birth."[9] He drew upon rather than tapped spiritual resources in his testing. In similar fashion, it seems correct to think of Jesus as quoting from a psalm depicting not only the struggle against pain but the triumph of faith over it.

Some years ago I visited an acquaintance who was in the hospital. He had a way of getting his points over in a startling fashion. I mentioned to him the opportunity of prayer, to which he responded: "I haven't prayed since I got into the hospital." He watched me for a moment to see what emotion I might betray, and then added: "I pray before illness, and trust during it." While his explanation was more categorical than his actual practice, he expressed rather well the resolution, the continuity of faith which sustained him.

---

[9] Abraham Cohen, *The Psalms*, p. 62.

PRAISE

At verse 22 the psalm takes an abrupt change in mood, followed by the admonition to men to praise God. It is as if a holy quietness has settled upon the turbulent soul to prepare the way for rejoicing. The believer knows this experience well. In the bitter experience he prays through to rest in the Lord and to songs of deliverance.

The author of Hebrews chose verse 22 (Heb. 2:12) along with two other texts to suggest the affinity of Christ to man in His death subsequent consolation (Heb. 2:9, 18). The crux of the argument is that Christ was tempted in His suffering ("suffered in His temptation" being a possible alternative) so that He might succor those who are similarly afflicted. By suffering He became the perfect author of salvation, bringing many sons to glory (Heb. 2:10). "He is the strong swimmer who carries the rope ashore and not only secures His own position but makes rescue for all who will follow."[10] Christ's words of comfort and confidence are not empty, because He has entered glory by the same path. Having suffered, He can console and direct those going through a similar experience.

Praise is not meant to be kept hidden. The psalmist's experience is intended as a token of grace for the sanctuary (vs. 25). His deliverance is a chapter for the book of God's faithful remembrance of His people. It will sustain others in their time of trouble. An offering of thanksgiving is to be made, and the people will join in the festivity (cf. Lev. 7:16 with vss. 25-26). The benediction of God is proclaimed upon all those of like faith.

Now the horizon of the psalm lifts to embrace all mankind (vss. 27-31). The nations will turn to Yahweh. He will be worshiped alike by those who have enjoyed the best of life, and those who were bowed to the dust by poverty and care (vs. 29). The universal appeal of the kingdom seems to suggest that the fact of suffering no longer will separate man from his fellow, but all will see the redemptive rationale of God's purpose with man. The stress on God's righteousness appears to confirm the intent (vs.

---

[10]Marcus Dodds, *The Epistle of the Hebrews, Expositor's Greek Testament,* IV, p. 265.

31). Protest is replaced by praise, a song of exaltation in which the peoples of the earth join.

The psalm closes with a grand contrast: instead of a cry for help, the shout of deliverance; instead of forsakenness, the acclaim of fulfillment; instead of question, the answer in hand. Nevertheless, the strand of faith runs throughout. At the very moment the psalmist lies in the dust of death, Yahweh's purpose is being realized through him (vs. 15).

PRÉCIS

"For now we see in a mirror dimly, but then face to face; now I know in part, but then I shall know fully just as I also have been fully known" (I Cor. 13:12). There is no more pertinent issue to which to apply this text than the problem of pain. The Christian accepts the reality of suffering in the light of his faith and confidence in God's redemptive purpose at work. We have further considered the nature of the experience which embodies the pain, and weighed against it the abiding reality of the fellowship of suffering.

The resolution of the problem is of necessity suggestive. We do not share omniscience with the Almighty. However, pain can be understood against the background of God's redemptive purpose and on the scene of spiritual conflict. It provides an opportunity to witness, both to man's affliction of his fellow and God's sustaining grace to the tormented. Suffering produces no automatic growth in Christian character; it is not in itself an effective testimonial to those observing. But it is an opportunity to be seized by the person who is open to receive "both good and evil" at God's hand, who will, with resolution fostered by the Christian walk, persevere through the testing.

Beyond the veil of tears is the bright day. The occasion of suffering seen in retrospect through God's sustaining grace and subsequent deliverance is the stuff of which praise is made. God is to be acknowledged in our this-worldly experience—through responsibility, suffering, and pleasure—rather than some other-worldly dream—escape, fantasy, retreat. We cannot reject the road which Christ walked, if we would share the crown which Christ won. The road leads through pain to praise.

7

Corporate Personality

A community provides not only a common ground of support but also protection against the out-group. The love of Christ, however, constrains the Church to lower its natural defenses and to risk its life in the cause of turning men to God. Such a dynamic deserves the title of travail.

Corporate Personality

A psalm of the Sons of Korah.   A Song.

1. On the holy mount he founded (it), (and)
2. Yahweh loves the gates of Zion more than the dwelling places of Jacob.
3. Glorious things are spoken of you, city of God.
4. I will proclaim Rahab and Babylon as those knowing Me. Behold, (of) Philistia and Tyre along with Ethiopia (it shall be said): "This one is born there."
5. And of Zion it shall be said: "This one and that one is born in her," and the Highest Himself will establish her.
6. The Lord records when registering the people: "This one is there." Selah.
7. As well singers and dancers (say): "All my fountains are in you."

PSALM 87

The term Zion (vs. 2) reflects more than a historic and troubled faith, or the special promises of God to the Hebrew people. It can be applied to Christian experience in general and the Church in particular. Here we will consider the latter application.

THEORY

Corporate personality means that an individual functions not in isolation from but in conjunction with others. It is recognition "of the fact that the individual is more than an atom cut off from his group; rather he as an individual is such because he is part of the group from which he emerges. It might be declared with slight modification that the group is a mass individual living through its constituent members."[1] The person is in part the result of the group, and bears in common with his associates certain basic characteristics of the group.

The corporate personality is not necessarily limited to geographical location or to a generation of people. The Hebrew partook of the social heritage of Abraham, Isaac, and Jacob by way of instruction and veneration. Edmund Fleg, reflecting on the question of why he was a Jew, observed: "And I say to myself: From this remote father [Abraham] right up to my own father, all these fathers have handed on to me a truth which flowed in their blood, which flows in mine; and shall I not hand it on, with my blood, to those of my blood?"[2]

There is a peculiar social character which identifies personality, whether corporate or individual. Corporate social character is that structure which is common to most members of the group. The individual deviates from the social character due to a variety of factors but he is still a representative of the body. Social character is necessarily more general than that of the individual, but it often provides the clue to understanding a person's response.

A social identity is forged through basic experience and a common mode of response. This can readily be illustrated from Israel's past. God did not forsake His people to the abuse of Egypt, but delivered them from Pharaoh, sustained them through

[1]Russell Shedd, *Man in Community*, p. 5.
[2]Arthur Hertzberg, *The Zionist Idea*, p. 485.

the wandering, and settled them in the promised country. For this reason the prophets consistently urged the people to thankfulness and restraint from idolatry. The corporate personality was being realized as a result of experience and the common attitude solicited in response. The rhapsodies which Zion called forth were due less to the walls which towered about it or the splendor of the Temple in the sun's reflection than to the corporate personality of a people with whom the Hebrew identified.

Sufficient background has been sketched to allow the stating of a thesis of sweeping implications: ideas are important only as they provide meaning in a social environ. Society is much more than suppression, as Freud implied, or the dialectical framework for economic interests as Marx claimed; it is the matrix where meaning is measured.

Man is not so much a being who relates as he is a being in relationship. He is perhaps the least self-sufficient of animal progeny, not only capable of culture but dependent upon it. From earliest memory his personal meaning is understood in the light of association with others. He sees himself reflected in the look, response, or creative silence of his fellows. He derives meaning in a qualified sense *from*, but in any case, *in* community.

The text now opens to us exciting possibilities. A little-employed psalm, it is perhaps the most remarkable entry in the Psalter. Its picture of God's purpose being realized with humanity is comparable to similar passages in Isaiah. Man is viewed as responding to divine summons and taking up residence in the city of God. The occasion of the psalm's writing has been variously understood as a national victory of some importance[3] or the

---

[3]The reference to Egypt and Babylon as dominant world powers, and parallels with Isaiah, have led numerous commentators to tie the psalm to Sennacherib's catastrophe (II Kings 18:13–19:37; II Chron. 32:1–22; Isa. 36:1–37:38). Sennacherib's annals picture earlier successes—the threat to Jerusalem, payment of tribute—but no reference to the destruction of his army: "As for Hezekiah, the Jew, who did not submit to my yoke, 46 of his strong, walled cities, as well as the small cities in their neighborhood, which were without number (succumbed) . . . . 200,150 people, great and small, male and female, horses, mules, asses, camels, cattle and sheep, without number, I brought away from them and counted as spoil. Himself, like a caged bird, I shut up in Jerusalem, his royal city." No claim is made for a siege, and Assyria's fortune declined rapidly, perhaps reflecting the defeat suffered.

reception of proselytes. It may be outlined as: theocracy, the rule of God (vss. 1-3); theodicy, the turning to God (vss. 4-7).

The importance of our consideration should be underscored before proceeding. Individual man varies from the character structure of his group, although this is best understood as a deviation from the nucleus. Up to this point our main interest has been to understand the individual more fully, and therefore we have given preference to personal considerations. "However, if we want to understand how human energy is channeled and operates as a productive force in a given social order then the social character deserves our main interest."[4]

THEOCRACY

Zion is described as "the city of God" (vs. 3). Yahweh has founded it (vs. 1), and esteems it above the villages of Israel (vs. 2). It is the habitat of His holiness (Jer. 31:23), and from it proceeds His law (Isa. 2:3). Zion is the corporate symbol for the people of God, the peculiar expression of God's domain.

The author of Hebrews employs Zion as the figure of the Church (Heb. 12:22-23). Paul speaks of the Church as participating in the promise made to the people of God (Israel) (Eph. 2:12-13), and of Christ being the foundation for "the dwelling of God" (Eph. 2:22). The Church is beloved (Eph. 5:25), and it is sustained through affliction (Eph. 3:13-16). It is the society of the reconciled, the being reconciled, and the reconciling (I Cor. 5:14-21). Here Christ has been professed, and is being preferred and pronounced to others. The Church is Christ in community, the society of divine rule.

There are four traditional marks applied to the Church: apostolicity, universality, unity, and sanctity. These signs have been generally stressed for formal and/or polemic reasons. While it is legitimate and profitable to approach the issue in these ways, we shall rather consider them for the interpersonal dynamic implied. Our hope is to uncover how the divine purpose becomes operative in the body of believers.

---

[4]Erich Fromm, "Character and the Social Process," *Theories of Personality* (Lindzey and Hall, eds.), p. 117.

Apostolicity

The discussion of apostolicity involves the authority exercised in regard to the community. No organized society is possible without authority. Divine authority is the recognized norm for the Church; God's word provides the needed unity and stability. In its response to the authority of God, the Church becomes the earnest of the theocracy—the Kingdom of God. "The Church . . . is the present manifestation of the Kingdom of God and in her the Kingdom's transforming power operates and from her its life and blessedness flows to form an oasis in the desert of this world's sin and misery, darkness and death, to which the thirsty traveler may come and drink deeply at the well-spring of salvation."[5]

The Church is not synonymous with the Kingdom of God, in either its present realization or its future expectation. Common grace precedes special grace, and provides the background and environment within which the latter operates. God *now* restrains evil in its means and from its destructive ends. He *now* supports constructive activity as it figures in the cultural mandate to subdue the earth. Government, home, and labor are aspects of God's order and indications of His authority.

There is also a future cosmic dimension to the Kingdom. The climactic intervention of Christ in the course of history is promised (I Thess. 4:16-17). He will receive the scepter of His reign (Rev. 11:15). The forces of evil will be eventually and permanently curtailed (Rev. 20:11-15), and the theocracy will be realized in cosmic fulness (I Cor. 15:28). For the present, the Church is the fellowship gathered to demonstrate the sovereignty of God and His gracious purpose toward man. The apostolic task is to communicate to others that which is received of Christ, to perpetuate the continuity of faith. The published word becomes the promise of reconciliation and the means of establishing Christian fellowship. The Church exists because it was called into being by the word and on the authority of God.

Universality

The second mark of the Church is illustrated by the familiar

---

[5]Raymond O. Zorn, *Church and Kingdom*, p. 81.

passage from the early Roman historian Tacitus: "Christus, the founder of that name [Christians], was put to death as a criminal by Pontius Pilate at the reign of Tiberius, but the pernicious superstition repressed for a time, broke out again not only throughout Judea, where the mischief originated, but also in the city of Rome."[6] The Church knows no boundaries, no locality, race, or social distinction. The gospel was to be proclaimed to all men (Matt. 24:14; 28:18-20; Luke 24:46-47). Within three decades from the death of Christ, the word had spread from Judea to Rome, and had embraced a "vast multitude," according to Tacitus' further elaboration.

Even more striking is the boast of Tertullian a century later: "We are but of yesterday and we have filled every place among you—cities, islands, fortresses, towns; market-places, the very camp, tribes, companies, palace, senate, forum . . . we have left nothing but the temples of your idols."[7] The Church welcomes every man, but not his vain images.

Nondifferentiation corresponds to universality as obedience does to authority. Like its Lord, the Church is no respecter of persons. In fact both value a purposeful variety, whether diversity in creation or the diverse ministries within the Church (I Cor. 12:14-25). The psalmist points to this high regard for variety; he describes the delight of God as He lists the names of those who have come from such various origins (vs. 4).

Unity

The Church is one (cf. vss. 1, 3, 6). It is a company of penitents who have put their trust in the Lord. This realization guards against prideful presumption and unhealthy criticism on the one hand, and fortifies against abandonment and despair on the other.

Paul Tournier describes the subtle dynamics of interpersonal criticism: "Thus in everyday life we are continually soaked in this unhealthy atmosphere of mutual criticism, so much so that we are not always aware of it and we find ourselves drawn unwittingly into an implacable vicious circle; every reproach evokes a feeling

---

[6]Tacitus, *Annales*, XX, 44.
[7]Tertullian, *Apologeticum*, 37.

of guilt in the critic as much as in the one criticized, and each one gains relief from his guilt in any way he can, by criticizing other people and in self-justification."[8] The Christian community should rather be a forgiving community, for it has experienced forgiveness. It can provide consolation, for it has been consoled in Christ.

It does not follow that the community will treat sin lightly. Paul demanded action on behalf of the Corinthian believers to rectify their evils (I Cor. 5). The very love which characterizes the Church requires that it stand against the sin which would destroy its members. However, the stance is redemptive. It does not boast over the fallen, recognizing the propensity in all to sin; it seeks to reclaim the erring.

The unity of faith also protects the believer from the despair which is natural to any man, and peculiarly to one receiving the immeasurably high calling in Christ. The sense of variance between Christian ideal and practice can be the cause of disabling guilt. Where an isolated person would succumb, the member of the Church may be sustained by the strength of the corporate personality. As in the case of an injury to one's physical body, protective and restorative resources are summoned from elsewhere to combat the difficulty.

Group theorists talk of *interstimulation*, the increase of central motion built up in an aggregation of persons developing unity. There is a gravitational-like hold which is exerted on those belonging to the group. How supremely this is true of those experiencing Christ's love in community!

Sanctity

The Church is called out from a world which has surrendered to its own depravity, which does not simply break the ordinances of God but gives hearty approval to those who are disobedient (Rom. 1:28-32). It is instructed to love God and repudiate affection for the world (I John 2:15). The Church is called not from life but from disobedience (I John 2:17).

The Church's head is Christ from whom its identity is taken.

---

[8]Paul Tournier, *Guilt and Grace*, pp. 15-16.

It accepts the servant role as did its Lord (Matt. 25:40). Its holiness reflects the compassion of God, and its nature the likeness of Christ.

The Church as a fellowship is far from perfect, and in its institutional form it includes false adherents (Matt. 13:21-30, 47-50). Time will disclose the truthfulness of faith and the perversity of fault. The community is to take appropriate action as its need is indicated, but not to become obsessed with rooting out the heretics. Otherwise, the tender faith of some will receive incalculable harm.

In conclusion, look at the strong masculine symbols of faith used by the psalmist: God is the builder, and Zion stands impregnable (vs. 1). Like other early Canaanite settlements, the original city of Jerusalem was situated on a rocky spur isolated on three sides by deep valleys. It was thereby suited to military defense and provided maximum security for its inhabitants. Great armies were stymied by the walls of Jerusalem towering above the valleys below.

However, the true strength of the city lay not in its advantageous location and supplementary defenses, but in the presence of God (vs. 3). For all of their natural security, the Israelites were terrified at the approach of the Assyrians. Isaiah could disdain the enemy because their advance was an affront to God. "Against whom have you raised your voice and haughtily lifted your eyes? Against the Holy One of Israel" (II Kings 19:22). Judah's success was assured because of the presence of the Defender, not because of the defense.

The Church has often been able to exert influence in an impressive, if not wise, fashion. Its affluence has threatened at times the stability of the state and conversely has been depleted out of resentment. The Church is weak in its own strength but strong in God. The counsel of evil is said not to be able to resist it (Matt. 16:18). For all its vulnerability, only the fool would despise the Church, the fellowship where God's name resides (vs. 3).

THEODICY

The psalmist turns now from the masculine image of Zion as an impregnable fortress to the feminine image of a receptive woman, impregnated by God's love to bring forth children of faith (vs. 4). From theocracy, the rule of God, we arrive at theodicy, conversion to Him.

Mother of the Nations

The discussion has turned on aggressiveness, rigor, and discipline—masculine qualities; but here the tone must be altered to allow the sensitivity and enrichment of feminine character. Anna Hempstead Branch's verse on her mother's words are appropriate to set the mood:

> My mother has the prettiest tricks
>   Of words and words and words.
> Her talk comes out as smooth and sleek
>   As breasts of singing birds.
>
> . . . .
>
> We had not dreamed these things were so
>   Of sorrow and of mirth.
> Her speech is as a thousand eyes
>   Through which we see the earth.
>
> God wove a web of loveliness,
>   Of clouds and stars and birds,
> But made not any thing at all
>   So beautiful as words.
>
> They shine around our simple earth
>   With golden shadowings,
> And every common thing they touch
>   Is exquisite with wings.
>
> There's nothing poor and nothing small
>   But is made fair with them.
> They are the hands of living faith
>   That touch the garment's hem.
>
> They are as fair as bloom or air,
>   They shine like any star,
> And I am rich who learned from her
>   How beautiful they are.

Such is the winsomeness of the Church's plea to man to be reconciled to God. It stresses the compassion of its Lord, reflected in a patient and painful endurance with a wayward people. It intuitively feels that distress which the prodigal cannot put into words, keeping the arms of invitation open for the repentant's return. Similarly, the Rabbinic commentary testifies: "The Holy One, praised be He, does not disqualify any creature; He accepts anyone. The gates are always open, and whoever wants to enter may enter."[9]

Travail of Birth

Love must conquer (Rom. 12:21). There is a natural resentment which must be overcome, the neutralizing of natural resistance to those who are different. "Narrow nationalistic pride could have crossed Philistia off the list, national jealousy could have refused to speak of Tyre, and racial snobbishness could have looked down on the teeming dark peoples of the land of Kush."[10] We tend to suspect the unfamiliar, recognizing in it a threat to our security. A community provides not only a common ground of support, but also protection against the out-group. The love of Christ, however, constrains the Church to lower its natural defenses and to risk its life in the cause of turning men to God. Such a dynamic deserves the title of travail.

The Church must overcome not only its own corporate resistance but also the hostility of the nations. How Israel had suffered at the hands of great and small alike! They had been torn like a scrap of meat thrown to the dogs. Antagonisms were deeply rooted. Not one or even several generations could hope to dissipate the suspicion and the stereotype. The Church is slow to recognize that it is held in contempt by a major percentage of the world's population. It is the opiate of the people to the communist world; to the Moslem masses it is the Crusades; to countless people the world over it is the symbol of Western colonization. The complaints of the protesting nations are largely justified. To face a world which disdains your existence is also travail.

---

[9] *Exodus Rabbah* 19:4. Quoted in Hertzberg, ed., *Judaism*, p. 34.
[10] Edwin McNeill Poteat, *The Interpreter's Bible*, IV, p. 470.

Perhaps the most difficult reality for the Church to face in its theodicy is apathy. A great segment of the world's population either gives lip service to the teaching of the Church or accepts it as one of the world religions. Christianity may be tolerated either for its assumed benefit or for its needed alliance. It is tolerated but its claims are not taken seriously. The Church can face its own limitation and the hostility of the nations better than the indifference of mankind. It can accept the role of martyr more easily than that of mediocrity. But there is no turning to God without the suffering of the Church. The child is conceived in love but born through travail.

Love which conquers is the product of community, the corporate personality of the Church. It calls upon all the resources of a redemptive fellowship in order to be actualized in the lives of its membership. It is threatened at every turn, but it must triumph in the purpose of God.

Rejoicing in the City

There is perhaps no bolder anthropomorphism in Scripture than that of God gleefully registering the people (vs. 6), taking a personal concern and delight in each one. A striking balance is maintained here between the community and the individual: "God does not desire a community which absorbs the individual into itself, but a community of men. In his sight the community and the individual are present at the same moment, and rest in one another."[11] God singles out the individual for attention, and inscribes his name on the city roster.

In the tension between the differentiation of persons and the dynamic of society, we can observe several concepts at work—the concepts of instinct, idea, and ideal. An instinct may be said to drive a man, an idea to pull him, but an ideal is a meaning which he realizes for himself. The ideal is the incarnation of idea into personality, the personal locus of meaning around which life is oriented. The city of God would degenerate quickly if uniformity were its goal. The variety of ideals within a community insures the continued vitality of the society. Through the dia-

---

[11]Dietrich Bonhoeffer, *The Communion of Saints*, p. 52.

logue of persons, each expressing his own ideals, there is formulated a growing sense of value and meaning.

The contrast between national origins in the psalm is apparently not meant to imply depreciation of the proselyte. The opposite may be the case. Because he lacks the natural inclination of the person nurtured in Zion, the proselyte should be commended for the very obstacles which he overcomes in embracing God's promise. A rabbinic comment is pertinent here: "A proselyte who has come of his own accord is dearer to God than all the Israelites who stood before Him at Mount Sinai. Had the Israelites not witnessed the thunders, lightnings, quaking mountains and sound of trumpets, they would not have accepted the Torah. The proselyte, who saw not one of these things, came and surrendered himself to the Holy One, praised be He, and took the yoke of Heaven upon himself. Can anyone be dearer to God than such a person?"[12] The Lord's parable on the lost sheep (Luke 15:1-7) shows that there is more rejoicing over that one than over the ninety-nine who were in the fold.

The parable of the prodigal son that follows the parable of the lost sheep is also relevant (Luke 15:11-32). The elder brother, representing incensed religious leaders, begrudged the feast given to the prodigal by his rejoicing father. He supposed that the prodigal's gain would be his loss. He poorly understood the nature of community where the true gain of one enriches all. In the sharing fellowship all benefit when one is acclaimed, and all are depreciated in the injury to any. For the psalmist, God's love was not diminished toward those born to Zion as the converts arrived from Egypt and Babylon. Instead there was joy unrestrained.

We have reflected on the motherlike love of the Church for the lost, the travail which it devoutly assumes to bring forth life, and the rejoicing which accompanies introduction into the family of God. Now the psalmist pauses as if out of reverence for the sanctity of the divine-human drama he has witnessed, before proceeding with the final refrain (vs. 7) in which the singers attest that man's resources are to be found in Zion.

---

[12]*Tanhuma, Lekh Lekha,* 6, quoted in Hertzberg, ed., *Judaism,* pp. 35-6.

THESIS

There is no dichotomy between self and society, but there are tensions, which are most adequately resolved in the Church. The Church as a corporate personality bears the marks of apostolicity, universality, unity, and sanctity. This is its evangelical nature. It also acts as the agency through which God brings to life those dead in trespasses. This is its evangelistic function. The Church is theocracy and theodicy, the *alpha* and *omega* of God's redemptive purpose with man. Origen reflected it all in his testimonial: "For the word, spoken with power, has gained mastery over men of all sorts of nature and it is impossible to find any race of men which has escaped the teachings of Jesus."[13]

Social identity is forged through experience and the fostering of a pattern of response. The Church's experience is with the sovereignty and redemptive activity of God. The terms "Lord" and "Savior" attributed to Christ correspond to these two aspects of experience.

The Church is coextensive with other units of society. Jesus Christ refused to draw the categorical distinction demanded by His questioners (Matt. 22:21). A Christian may be an American, a Republican, a member of the C.I.A., and so on, but the fact that he is a Christian will define to some degree the extent, and in every sense the nature, of his other involvements. He welcomes the opportunity to work cooperatively with others in constructive social enterprise, but is persuaded that Christ is the Mediator (I Tim. 2:5). While this conviction does not curtail his ministry, it will play a critical role in setting priorities and suggesting ways of implementing decisions and goals.

The social gospel is not a substitute for the good news of salvation, but the gospel is social. Once the believer has found the place of God's will in society, he is at the point of divine opportunity. Here he can mediate the purpose of God to men where they live, where truth is relevant.

---

[13]Origen, *Contra Celsum*, II, 13.

— 8 —

The Meaning
of Prayer

Prayer is not introduction to bondage but an invitation
to freedom. . . . The disciple prays that his creative
powers may be developed to the full in order to cope
with the complex order of events which confront him. . . .
There are few more exciting prospects to discipleship
than the kind of sanctified brainstorming implied here.

The Meaning of Prayer

To the choir director.   A psalm of David.

1. (May) Yahweh answer you in the day of trouble. The name of the God of Jacob protect you,
2. Send you help from the sanctuary, and assist you from Zion.
3. (May He) remember all your offerings, and be pleased with your sacrifices. Selah.
4. (May He) grant you according to your heart and fulfill all your counsel.
5. We shall acclaim your deliverance, and in the name of our God set up a banner. (May) Yahweh fulfill all your petitions.
6. Now I know that Yahweh will deliver His anointed. He will answer from His holy heaven, with powerful deliverance by His right hand.
7. Some (boast) of chariots and some of horses, but we remember the name of Yahweh our God.
8. They are brought down and fallen, but we rise and stand upright.
9. Deliver the king, Yahweh, answer us in the day we call.

PSALM 20

Prayer precedes any apologetic for its use. The psalmist no more questions the need of prayer than he questions the existence of God. Yet we are faced at every turn with criticism, particularly concerning the type of petition which assumes the possible alteration of physical law. Pain and drought are said to result from physical causes rather than moral appeals. Prayer relieved of such consideration, while perhaps of less offense to contemporary thought, seems to lack something of Biblical reality. This dilemma hovers like a spectre over our consideration of the subject.

EXPERIENTIAL CONTEXT

The psalm is not a treatise on prayer. It is a petition on behalf of a king, likely in preparation for conflict. There is intercession (vss. 1-5), assurance of God's deliverance (vss. 6-8), and concluding supplication (vs. 9). What we may learn of prayer we must find largely in an indirect fashion. Yet, while there is little formal treatment of the subject, the text breathes with the existential reality of prayer.

Prayer as Natural

Prayer is apparently accepted as a natural expression of man, the reflection of a dimension of his personality. Absence of prayer may be as much abnormality as impiety: "Therefore the only monstrosity of nature, just as much a monstrosity as a wingless fish, is the prayerless man or woman, because the deepest and most real instinct is not satisfied."[1] Prayer marks the being created for communion with God.

Today, however, the advent of secularization has been announced, and with it a new norm for human experience. Harvey Cox characterizes the advent as "the loosing of the world from religious and quasi-religious understandings of itself, the dispelling of all closed world-views, the breaking of all supernatural myths and sacred symbols."[2] He proceeds to distinguish between sec-

[1] James Hastings (ed.), *The Doctrine of Prayer*, p. 3.
[2] Harvey Cox, *The Secular City*, p. 2.

ularization, an irreversible historical process by which society is delivered from servitude to religious and metaphysical world-views, and secularism, a new closed view which functions similarly to religion. Secularization, Cox says, has developed in large measure from the formative influence of Biblical faith.

Cox has a point. There is a sense in which Genesis is a form of "atheistic propaganda," the divesting of the universe of the divine. The Christian Deity is not a nature god, but the God of nature. The sharpest differentiation is made between the Creator and His creation. There is a natural world, and if prayer is to be, it must be seen as a phenomenon related to the natural order.

Prayer concerns real things. Some have thought that the psalm reflects David's expedition against Syria (II Sam. 8:4-5; 10:15-19). In any case, it is not polite conversation but urgent appeal. Prayer is distorted where natural events are not taken seriously. It is communication born of sensed need.

Prayer as *Supernatural*

The world does not exist as a self-contained framework of meaning. Christianity synthesizes the natural into a more comprehensive explication of life. Prayer, too, must be understood within the larger context of understanding.

Cox is correct in his estimation that Christianity repudiates "life in an enchanted forest," where reality is "charged with a magical power that erupts here and there to threaten or benefit man. Properly managed and utilized, this invisible energy can be supplicated, warded off, or channeled."[3] But Cox seems to confuse the nature of the Biblical distinction and therefore accepts rather uncritically the arrival of the secular city.

Eugene Nida assists us at this juncture. In a prepared lecture he developed extensively the difference between superstition and the supernatural. The former has to do with an essentially mechanistic universe which can be manipulated by skill. The latter is a personal world where man is understood to be morally responsible. The Scripture disavows the superstitious, but is candidly supernaturalistic.

[3]*Ibid.*, p. 21.

Prayer is best understood as the soul of worship. God, rather than creation, is the subject of supreme worth. He is not the impersonal ground of being but the personal object of faith. The basic idea of prayer "is that of two-way communication, call and response of some sort, or, as we might term it, genuine personal fellowship."[4] The psalmist employs the personal name of God (vss. 1, 5, 7, 9); Jesus stressed the most intimate of designations—"our Father." The believer finds the worship of brick and mortar little improvement over that of wood and stone, and a poor substitute for the living God. Praying man is in communion.

3 Prayer as Operational

Prayer is the handmaiden of responsibility. It is asking God to "bless our own efforts and labors and make them effective insofar as they can be effective and to add to them when they must be supplemented."[5] The believer realizes the need both of enabling grace in his own efforts, and of extended grace in regard to God's overruling providence. His concern in prayer is to be available for God's use in realizing His purpose (vs. 2).

The form of pietism which curtails creative thought and purposeful action and calls such curtailing the will of God must rank among the chief offenses. An asinine act turns into blasphemy when perpetrated in the name of God. Prayer not only prescribes that man shall act, but that he act wisely. "The only causes . . . for which we may fight are those which we can take into God's house; the only swords we can draw are those which we can lay on the altar."[6] Praying man is to act responsibly.

We have come to understand the context of prayer by the accident of life, the availability of God, and the accountability of man. Several questions are related. Does prayer perpetuate the infancy of man? Does God really alter the physical order? Can man have thorough confidence in the exercise of prayer? We shall consider these questions in order.

The need which urges prayerfulness is not to be thought of as

[4] Winston King, *Buddhism and Christianity, Some Bridges of Understanding,* p. 24.
[5] Fred Fisher, *Prayer in the New Testament,* p. 77.

an infant dependence but as the critical stress arising from growth and action. "If true prayer sometimes springs from weakness, it is at least from willingness, with the realization that unaided one will find it difficult to advance from weakness to strength."[7] Jesus' life was the most adequate ever lived, but He resorted periodically to prayer. Luke's Gospel in particular is careful to point out how Jesus armed Himself with prayer when approaching the critical decisions of life.

The maturing Christian finds that his need for prayer is not lessened, but that the subject and nature of prayer is altered. He realizes that certain victories may be claimed, and that he can go on to *new* tasks and challenges. He also discovers that his prayers tend to become less self-centered and self-seeking. The needs of others and his concern to be of help replaces the obsession with his own frailty. The mature pray differently but, as they are sensitive to their needs, with renewed urgency.

A related issue concerns the idea of God altering physical forces, and here the Christian does well not to limit the way in which the Almighty may choose to work. George Müller described as the prime motive in his orphanage work "to have something to point to as a visible proof that our God and Father is the same faithful God that he ever was—as willing as ever to prove himself the living God, in our day as formerly, to all that put their trust in him."[8] His experience illustrates the diversity and creativity of God's work, rather than prescribing a pattern which all must follow.

A final question has to do with man's confidence in prayer. Faith requires encouragement. The psalmist's reference to "the name" (vs. 1) is meant to remind the listeners of the nature of the Person. All analogy drawn from human relationship breaks down because of man's finiteness and failure. Simply to allow "the name" to pass one's lips is an invitation to believe.

Yahweh is particularized as "the God of Jacob" (vs. 1). The Talmud has what at first seems to be a rather novel explanation of

[6]J. R. P. Sclater, *The Interpreter's Bible*, IV, p. 109.
[7]Horatio Dresser, *Outlines of the Psychology of Religion*, p. 60.
[8]*The Life of Trust*, p. 126.

the title, but which reflects the pious wisdom of the sages: "The God of Jacob and not the God of Abraham and Isaac? This teaches that the owner of the beam should go in with the thickest part of it."[9] The reasoning is that one puts the thicker end of a beam to the ground to provide better support, and Jacob is the more immediate ancestor of the Jewish people. The lesson is that encouragement is best mediated through those closest to us.

In any case, prayer is the mark of a maturing individual, aware of his responsibility and the availability of God. While realizing that his effectiveness is less than complete, the disciple is confident that the Almighty can take much less than the desired response and turn it to good ends. The Christian's experience is far removed from the enchanted forest, but it transcends with marked contrast the cycle of despair and ill-founded optimism of the secular city.

EXAMPLES OF PETITION

While the nature of prayer is dialogue, its basic thrust takes the form of petition. Man calls to God out of need to enable him to further divine purpose. We shall reflect on those petitions which make up the first division of the psalm (vss. 1-5), and consider at the same time the teaching of the Disciples' Prayer (Matt. 6:9-15).

The petition for audience (vs. 1). The first petition appropriately recognizes the sovereignty of God and that as subject, man awaits the divine Ruler's summons. Similarly, Jesus spoke of God's special habitat as heaven, reminding us of His transcendent majesty and power. V. Raymond Edman never seemed to tire of telling of his experience of being received by Emperor Haile Selassie of Ethiopia, likening it to an audience with the King of kings. This favorite topic of worship as an audience with a king was on his lips when he collapsed in the pulpit of the Wheaton College Chapel named for him, and was ushered into the presence of God.

Dr. Edman used to describe not only the necessary respect required for royalty, but the deep interest expressed by the Em-

---

[9] *Berakoth*, 64a. *The Babylonian Talmud.*

peror in him and his work. So Christ taught His disciples to use the ascription "our Father" as a reminder of God's concern for each person separately and for the community of faith corporately.

2.   *The petition for protection* (vs. 1). "God is our refuge and strength, a very present (well-proved) help in trouble. Therefore, we will not fear though the earth should change, though the mountains tremble with its tumult. Selah" (Psa. 46:1-3). The psalmist turns to God in the time of crisis, reflecting not simply the urgency of the situation but the moral issue involved. The holiness of God precludes any other possibility than God's help. Only the man whose values are in heaven can pray for God's will to be done on earth.

Ernest Ligon reminds us that it is easy to "pray with deep piety for God's will to be done, and then refuse to spend any time at all finding out what it is."[10] The devotee of any enterprise must accept the responsibility of perfecting his vocation. The teachings of Scripture are the guidelines which provide the content for otherwise meaningless words.

3   *The petition for assistance* (vs. 2). Man is normally God's instrument for blessing. The disciple prays that the heavenly power may be available for his earthly ministry. His petition is task-centered but heaven-conscious. He recognizes the danger of assuming his wishes to be right, and earnestly attempts to perceive the will of God.

The prayer for assistance does not lessen but increases obligation. Sacrifice is called forth by service. The effort needed to maintain the *status quo* is comparatively slight, but that required to achieve some new success is demanding. Similarly, to pray for "our daily bread" is to assume a responsibility in regard not only to one's own needs but to that of his fellows. These words, so often uttered selfishly, are intended to bind the disciple in Christian concern to those in need.

We observe that petition has a way of opening man to the world to be served. It is a means of releasing life to the control of God. Progress is initiated by petition. The importance of being

---

[10]Ernest Ligon, *The Psychology of Christian Personality*, p. 201.

relentless in prayer (Luke 18:1) becomes evident at this point.
The petition for absolution (vs. 3). As the disciple sees his
responsibility, he becomes painfully aware of how far short of
spiritual capacity he has come. The language of the psalm takes
on that of the sacrificial ritual (cf. Lev. 2:2); the disciple prays
that his life might be as a living offering employed by God to His
purpose (Rom. 12:1).

Within the context of service it is much easier to understand the
disciple's request, "Forgive us our debts, as we have forgiven our
debtors" (Matt. 6:12). Forgiveness of others is not the formal
ground for divine forgiveness, but the life-dynamic of reconciliation. He who accepts the road of service finds obstacles of human
resentment and hostility. His ministry involves not only returning
good for evil, but forgiveness for persecution and love for hate.
His approximation of the Christian ideal is less than perfect, and
the disparity weighs heavily upon him. In this state of concern,
he prays for the forgiveness of God, even as he seeks to forgive
those who offend him.

The petition for creative imagination (vs. 4). Prayer is not an
introduction to bondage but an invitation to freedom. It "is the
voice of one who was created free, although he was born in
chains; it is at once self-assertion and self-surrender; *it claims a
will even in surrendering it*, when it says, 'Not my will, but Thine,
be done.' . . . Prayer is God's acknowledgment, His endorsement
of His own gift of freedom to man: it is His royal invitation . . .
to man to exert this privilege, to use this power."[11] Purposefully,
the disciple prays that his creative powers may be developed to
the full in order to cope with the complex order of events which
confront him. No set way of applying divine principles can be
allowed. The disciple must create priorities and means to make
available the grace of God.

There are few more exciting prospects to discipleship than the
kind of sanctified brainstorming implied here. Man ceases to be
an automaton and functions as the creative being which he was
intended to be. Implied are the need of personal and group
flexibility, the realization that one is part of a dynamic interplay

[11] Dora Greenwell and P. T. Forsyth, *The Power of Prayer*, pp. 24-25.

of forces, an openness to life and its possibilities, and a stability of faith which keeps the disciple from being swayed by every shift of public sentiment.

The petition for specific tasks (vs. 5). Prayer must become pointed. It has to go beyond a vague request for success to a particular occasion and specific means. C. S. Lewis's clever demonic figure Screwtape thought an effective way to frustrate one's prayer life was to keep prayer "spiritual," unrelated to the real situation. So he instructed the junior tempter to make his human subject separate his imagined from his real mother so that "no thought or feeling from his prayers for the imagined mother will ever flow over into his treatment of the real one."[12] The way to frustrate such diabolical planning is by directing prayer to reality in its most concrete form.

Once again we see that the Christian ideal offers no escape from responsibility but provides the means of creatively handling a given situation. The undertaking is nonetheless plagued with problems. Man is sorely tempted to abuse his abilities, to turn his constructive potential to destructive ends. The disciple prays that he might escape this snare (Matt. 6:13). He is also tempted to despair of the strenuous road of discipleship, and so prays that grace may enable him to persevere.

The Christian life must never become stagnant. The tasks which the disciple faces remind him of the need of further growth. He prays for deliverance, not from the arena of evil, but from its domination (Matt. 6:13); not for escape but for effectiveness.

We have considered the petitions in order. They are like a flower opening to the sunlight of God's love and blooming to His glory. They reject the concept of *Deus ex machina* (God out of the machine), the recourse to God to resolve those issues for which man hesitates to accept responsibility. The petitions rather reflect the awakening of man to accountability and to the grace of God as available to support him in assuming his creative and active role.

_____

[12]C. S. Lewis, *The Screwtape Letters*, pp. 21-22.

EFFECTIVE PRAYER

Prayer is ascribed to Yahweh, the living and self-revealing One, and is prescribed by His nature. Prayer is not at all effective in the sense of being able to manipulate divine justice, but it is essential in determining the means of its operation. Therefore, prayer is best thought of as communal, its effectiveness lying in the divine-human dialogue rather than in some rite which would obligate God to a prescribed course of action.

The man of faith is committed to the moral purpose of God. He is assured that in the long run righteousness exalts and sin degenerates (vss. 7-8). The fortunes of life change, but the obligation to responsibility remains unaltered. In this realization, Tertullian warned the Christian against obsession over recognition. "Never mind the state horses with their crown. Your Lord, when . . . He would enter Jerusalem in triumph, had not even an ass of His own. These (put their trust) in chariots, and these in horses; but we will seek our help in the name of the Lord our God."[13] Cyprian similarly encouraged believers during trial: "Wherefore in persecution let no one think what danger the devil is bringing in, but let him indeed consider what help God affords; not let human mischief overpower the mind, but let divine protection strengthen the faith."[14] Effective prayer remains resolute to the person and purpose of God. It is tenacious in its determination, neither relaxed nor discouraged by the changing circumstances of life (Luke 18:1).

Prayer must be experienced. It loses too much in the translation to be grasped otherwise. The confidence of the psalmist (vss. 6-8) came as a result of praying (vss. 1-5). He began with knowledge of a personal God (vs. 1) and realization of His presence (vs. 3), and through experience in prayer he came to confidence in His sustaining grace. Those who are persuaded pray, but those who are not refrain from prayer. Effective prayer is not formal but existential, not conceptualized but realized. It is born out of faith applied to situation.

---

[13]Tertullian, *The Chaplet*, XIII, 21-27.
[14]Cyprian, *The Treatises*, X, 65-70.

An individual needs a certain equilibrium in order to function properly. Chaos reaps confusion. Prayer has a function in integrating the personality around an ideal structure. It provides the means of reflection on and adaptation of aspects of life to those values thought important. Similarly, prayer stabilizes the aspirations, allowing psychical energies to be expended along more clearly defined channels. Prayer molds an organism into a person.

Prayer not only assists in orientation but also in acceptance of the self. For the Christian, this involves being a son of God (Rom. 8:14, 19; Phil. 2:15; I John 3:1-2), and results in a reverence for life. In realizing that he is valued, the disciple learns to value himself and others.

Prayer gives direction. The developing life is active. Each response to a challenge leaves the person better able to meet successive challenges. Prayer provides the vision necessary to order events in keeping with long-range goals. It solicits the courage to face difficult tasks. It revives the spirit to meet the demands of life. Prayer is the means of stabilizing the individual, achieving self-acceptance, and giving direction.

Effective prayer has been defined in connection with the nature and purpose of God, the experience of man, and the fulfillment of life. It is inexorably tied to the kingdom of God. When man advances "beyond the Santa Claus stage of prayer he will be asking for the secrets of transforming personality, for insight into the nature of the kingdom of heaven, and for knowledge of how this kingdom can be brought about on earth."[15] These are extending concerns for which only prayer has the length of reach.

ENTREATY FOR THE KING

The psalm concludes with an intercession for the king (vs. 9). Where the earlier petitions had to do with the undertaking of the leader, this verse concerns his office. What may be implied concerning prayer for those in authority?

The Christian is directed to be subject to those in authority (Rom. 13:1-7), and is specifically enjoined to bear them up in

---

[15]Ligon, op. cit., p. 191.

prayer (I Tim. 2:1-3). The latter injunction might well have been written during the barbarous rule of Nero, and certainly reflects a time of stress. Yet, the Christian is urged to pray for those who rule over him. He is to pray for serenity, godliness, and respect for the man with authority (I Tim. 2:2), implying several guidelines for his prayer concern.

Person

An authority figure is still a person and subject to the same compassion extended to others. We feel a peculiar ambivalence toward those in authority, since they are the symbols both of protection and of threat to our autonomy. Either view or both together tend to depersonalize the authority figure. "He-is-to-me" replaces the distinctive "he is." The person is no longer accepted as a subject, but as a means of organizing society. No doubt something of this sort is not only necessary but good. The problem arises when the person is emptied of his humanity and only the office remains. He becomes equivalent to his role.

The concern of Paul for tranquility of the ruler is in sharp contrast to the depersonalization of the authority figure. Prayer must encompass not only the functions of office but the facts of human personality. It must embrace the person who is performing the service.

Purpose

God's injunction is to be universally applied; man is to be subject to and solicitous of all authority: "To every one, whom we know to be placed in authority over us by his appointment, we should render reverence, obedience, gratitude, and all the other services in our power. Nor does it make any difference, whether they are worthy of this honour, or not."[16] The person in authority is subject to God, whether he cares to be or not, or whether he is aware of the fact or not. He will give account of the responsibility committed to his care.

Much is required of those to whom much is given (Luke

---

[16]John Calvin, *Institutes of the Christian Religion*, II, 8:35.

12:48). The authoritative role is not to be coveted but rather accepted with reverence. The Christian recognizes the rights and obligations of government in prayer. He esteems the office for the potential of good which it holds. He is reluctant to disparage the man in office, except in the most constructive fashion, for fear that in so doing he may undermine the very nature of authority itself. Chaos is no substitute for injustice.

Power

Paul admonishes us to pray for the godliness of those who rule. The psalmist reminds us that no authority is immune to the disposition and concern of God (vs. 9). The kingdoms of this world are under the judgment of the Almighty.

Prayer is not passive, as we have seen. The Christian clarifies in prayer the course of constructive support, the point and means of creative criticism, and the occasion when he may have to reject the demands of authority in the Name of a Greater One. As Bonhoeffer has been reported to have said: "It is not only my task to look after the victims of madmen who drive a motorcar in a crowded street, but to do all in my power to stop their driving at all."

Responsible citizenship is the ideal of pious reflection. The Kingdom is already being realized where the will of God is recognized as normative. The Christian senses the divine pulse in human society. He is more a citizen of this world for being a pilgrim toward the next.

Authority is good; only in its abuse is it evil. The Christian supports the person in authority, his role as an official, and the place of authority within the larger demands of the Kingdom. He renders reverence, obedience, and gratitude to those who accept on his behalf and before God the fearful task of leadership. Prayer is indicative of his commitment, illustrative of his concern, and effective in determining the nature of his creative support.

EPITOME

Prayer often seems strange and strained to contemporary man.

Part of the reason for this is that prayer is wrongly conceived as a means of manipulating God or retarding the *Deus ex machina.*

Properly conceived, prayer is intrinsic to responsible living. It is a divine-human dialogue concerning the expanding horizons of service. Prayer is more urgent than it ever was, and more demanding on the petitioner. It reflects the cooperation of man with his Maker. God does not cease to labor when man accepts more of his responsibility, but perhaps we can think of Him as increasing His endeavors. Every responsible act by man calls into being more of divine promise.

Petition is the sharp edge of prayer. Here man identifies the issues and develops his potential to cope with them. In petition he locates the resources of God by way of application to real situations. Petition strips dialogue of its niceties and gets down to critical concerns. It is the mark of man discovering meaning.

Effective prayer adequately grasps and reflects the great dialogue. It places one foot on the eternal purpose of God and the other in the changing arena of human activity. It activates the resources of communion rather than discussing the possible merits. Effective prayer both makes possible and is enriched by facing life together with the Almighty.

Prayer is socially sensitive, observing that social structure is necessary to man and good in God's sight. Prayer clarifies the nature of obligation and the means by which the Christian seeks to serve God *within* the society of which he is inevitably a part. Prayer is power, both to the individual and to the society of men.

9

Martial Challenge

Christianity must never be less than humanism, the be-
lief that man is somehow the measure of all things. It
will wage a ceaseless warfare toward realizing this elu-
sive goal. Every foe of man is an enemy of God, and
opposition to God is in the last analysis a threat to man.

Martial Challenge

To the choir director.
A Maskil of David, when Doeg the Edomite came and told
Saul: "David has come to the house of Ahimelech."

1. Why do you boast of wickedness, mighty man? The mercy of God (persists) every day.
2. Your tongue devises slander, like a sharp razor working deceit.
3. You love evil more than good, lying than telling the truth. Selah.
4. You love all devouring words, deceitful tongue.
5. God will also demolish you utterly. He will snatch and tear you from your tent, and shall uproot you from the land of the living. Selah.
6. But the righteous see, fear and laugh at him:
7. "Behold the man that would not make God his defense, but trusted in abundance of riches and sought defense in his self-will."
8. But I am like a green olive tree in the house of God.
9. I will praise You forever, because You accomplished it, and I will hope in Your name, for it is good in the sight of Your holy ones.

PSALM 52

The previous discussion concluded with commendation and resolute support of authority, but this psalm begins with an incrimination and implied resistance. Scriptural metaphors further suggest militancy, the experience of the godly illustrates it, and Christ makes it explicit: "Do not think that I have come to bring peace on earth. I have not come to bring peace, but the sword" (Matt. 10:34). God does not allow evil to go unchallenged, either directly or indirectly through his followers. The Christian is enlisted in a conflict of universal proportion.

CHRIST AND CULTURE

The arena of Christian combat is culture, the total process of human activity, the secondary environment superimposed upon the natural world. It involves at least ideology, language, custom, social structure, composite inheritance, and technical skill. Man is responsible for turning material things to divine ends. He is both aided and hindered in his task by the manner in which culture has been realized.

Christ as Telos *(Fulfillment) of Culture*

It is not surprising that radically different views concerning Christ and culture should have evolved. Some have tended to overlook the tension between the two, and to make Christ the hero of human history, the cultural triumph of the ages. Seventeenth- and eighteenth-century rationalism is a case in point. John Locke asserted that the teachings of Christ might be according to or above reason, but never contrary to it. Christ, he said, draws together the fragmented insights of man into the full revelation of God. In Him "morality has a sure standard, that revelation vouches, and reason cannot gainsay, nor question; but both together witness to come from God the great law-maker. An such an one as this, out of the New Testament, I think the world never had, nor can any one say, is any-where else to be found."[1] The revelation of Christ goes beyond reason, but the reasonable man can hardly reject His claims.

[1] John Locke, *The Reasonableness of Christianity*, p. 231.

The so-called "Social Gospel movement" had a similar tendency to eliminate the tension between Christ and culture. The social gospel was a creation of American Protestantism in its effort to resolve problems arising from the industrial and social revolution of the nineteenth century. Washington Gladden in his Lyman Beecher Lectures described God's role in social ferment: "In all this industrial struggle he is present in every part of it, working according to the counsel of his perfect will. In the gleams of light which sometimes break forth from the darkness of the conflict we discern his inspiration; in the stirrings of good-will which temper the wasing strife we behold the evidence of his presence; in the sufferings and losses and degradations which wait upon every violation of his law of love we witness the retribution with which that law goes armed."[2] Social crusade having become roughly synonymous with Christianity, Christ was installed as its high priest.

The efforts to seek an unconditioned peace between Christ and culture have generally been rejected both by the world and by the people of the Way. The reasonableness of Christianity did not commend itself any more to the "age of reason" than did Christian social rationale to the masses caught in revolutionary change. The Church likewise was suspect by those who minimized the importance of theology, stressed by law over grace, and seemed to distort the nature of historic Christianity.

Christ as Critic of Culture

Separation is the opposite pole from uncritical participation, and has been given a more persistent hearing in the Church. Regardless of the achievement recognized in man's societal attainment, he is required to choose between Christ and culture. Tertullian naturally comes to mind as soon as this position is mentioned. An articulate speaker of the second century, Tertullian was eventually led by the direction of his logic and the strength of his zeal away from the mainstream of Christianity into the moral perfectionism and apocalyptic speculations of Montanism.

---

[2]Washington Gladden, *Social Salvation*, p. 26.

His attitude toward culture is reflected in his attack on pagan entertainment: "Grant that you have there things that are pleasant, things both agreeable and innocent in themselves; even some things that are excellent. Nobody dilutes poison with gall and hellebore: the accursed thing is put into condiments well seasoned and of sweetest taste. So, too, the devil puts into the deadly draught which he prepares, things of God most pleasant and most acceptable."[3] Tertullian goes on to liken the edifying aspects of entertainment to honey dropped on a poisoned cake. The Christian must preclude its pleasures because of the evil distraction involved.

Isolation is implied in separation, and it has left the Church with an uneasy conscience while soliciting the criticism of the world for its apparent indifference. In fact, the radical divorcement of Christianity from culture always seems to reflect some pagan influence such as the stoicism in Tertullian. Grace is extracted from love; the monastic is saved while the world is allowed to go unchecked toward oblivion. Even if it were thought the right thing to do, isolation from culture is impossible. The very words used to preach separation are themselves facets of culture. Christ can no more be divorced from culture than He can be merged with it.

A PERSISTING ISSUE

There are, to be sure, mediating solutions which have been offered. One of these is the attitude assumed by Martin Luther as a result of criticism against his hard policy on the peasants' revolt. He responded: "God's kingdom is a kingdom of grace and mercy, not of wrath and punishment. In it there is only forgiveness, consideration for one another, love, service, the doing of good, peace, joy, etc. But the kingdom of the world is a kingdom of wrath and severity."[4] Two sets of demands were made upon the Christian, those of the heavenly and the earthly kingdoms. These reflected two moralities, necessarily accommodated to the

---

[3]Tertullian, *The Shows*, ch. 27.
[4]Martin Luther, "An Open Letter Concerning the Hard Book Against the Peasants," *Works of Martin Luther*, IV, p. 265.

events of life but still in tension. While Luther distinguished the two kingdoms, he did not divide them. The ideal was to make the best of the popular situation, to endure by God's grace the contradiction of experience.

Thomas Aquinas attempted a closer harmony, lessening the tension by subsuming all things under a divine overview.[5] This position provided a theoretical solution, but tended toward a practical compromise with culture.

Augustine illustrates the conversionist approach to culture, seeing Christianity primarily as a catalyst, a means of accelerating the divine purpose for mankind. He reasons: "In the universe, even that which is called evil, when it is regulated and put in its own place, only enhances our admiration of the good; for we enjoy and value the good more when we compare it with the evil. For the Almighty God, who, as even the heathen acknowledge, has supreme power over all things, being Himself supremely good, would never permit the existence of anything evil among His works, if He were not so omnipotent and good that He can bring good even out of evil."[6] Conversion occurs in, rather than apart from, the tension between Christ and culture, and is part of the process of resolution. Such a position naturally breeds an optimism which is only in a qualified sense supported by the facts of the case.

H. Richard Niebuhr, having examined the typical answers to the Christ and culture issue in much more detail, admits that the problem is unconcluded and inconclusive. However, he does suggest that a viable option must be relative and responsible: "Our decisions are individual, that is true; they are not individualistic—as though we made them for ourselves and by ourselves as well as in ourselves."[7] Decision reflects concern for the will of God and respect for the community of faith.

It is at this place, where Niebuhr locates the issue, that the psalmist takes his point of departure.

---

[5]Thomas Aquinas, *Summa Theologica*, II/I, Question 91, Third Article.
[6]Augustine, *Enchiridion*, ch. 11.
[7]H. Richard Niebuhr, *Christ and Culture*, p. 243.

ANALYSIS

The body of the text may be outlined as perspective on an enemy (vss. 1-4), prophecy of his destruction (vss. 5-7), and the happy prospect of those who trust in God (vss. 8-9). Its preface suggests the setting of the psalm, and the first division describes the experience of the psalmist.

Setting of the Psalm

David, in flight from Saul, was welcomed by the priest Ahimelech, who provided him with holy bread for sustenance and Goliath's sword for protection. Doeg the Edomite, having observed what transpired, slipped off to bring report of it to Saul. Ahimelech was charged with conspiracy. Rejecting his pleas of innocence, the king demanded that the priests and their families be put to death, a sentence subsequently carried out by Doeg (I Sam. 22). The inhumanity of this spiteful act provided the burden of the psalm.

The abuse of justice by arrogant magistrates remained a persisting problem for Israel, and called forth repeated warnings from the prophets. While the original offender may have been Saul, or Doeg as his emissary, "the wicked man . . . is apparently a type or generalization of a class rather than a specific individual, and the fate of such a man is compared with that of the godly man."[8] The original setting became an archetype for succeeding injustices.

Experience of the Psalmist

What was violated by this carnage (vs. 1)? It is both the humanistic dream and the divine revelation: "The humanist contends for the dignity of the human soul, refusing any dependence even upon God; the orthodox contends for the majesty of God, refusing any virtue which is not in God and wholly dependent upon him. The New Testament knows neither of these two extremes, although isolated texts could be picked for both."[9] The

---

[8]William R. Taylor, *The Interpreter's Bible*, IV, p. 273.
[9]E. H. Robertson, *Man's Estimate of Man*, pp. 81-2.

term repeatedly used of this ideal is *theonomy*, that which is at the same time the purpose of God and the perfection of man.

The blood-stained scene of the dead and dying depicts the frustration of God's noble plan for man. It is like an eruption of the evil which man harbors in his being, a blemish on humanity. The psalmist's emotion is repulsion, shock at the wrong performed, and fear for the man who does not fear for himself. It is a revulsion springing from reverence.

Shock is coupled with shame. There is a satirical bitterness and an ironic twist in the honorific title of "hero" ("mighty man," vs. 1) applied to an unworthy person. The magistrate who has been charged with the justice of all has himself violated the trust. He is like a deceitful tongue, all disparity between pretention and practice (vs. 4). His tongue is like a sharp razor, carefully sharpened for its slanderous occupation, skillfully apt for its invidious work (vs. 2). Nor are his actions unpremeditated or the result of some political necessity, for there is a heart propensity toward evil (vs. 3). Given a choice between the good and bad, he will choose the latter for no other reason than preference.

Shame is shock tolerated and perpetuated, the aversion which follows revulsion. It is resentment born of humiliation. While the hero boasts his evil exploits among his fellows, the psalmist cringes at the thought (vs. 1). Shame disturbs his peace and incites him to action.

Sedition follows on the heels of shame; the psalm has all the indications of insurrection. It has been called "a song of revolution." "Remember Nob" may well have become as much a rallying cry as "Remember the Maine" was in the Spanish-American conflict.

We have traced the psalmist's experience from human misery to militancy. The text, coupled with the record of David's reluctance to retaliate, is adequate testimony that all conciliatory efforts were being exhausted. The magistrate had not only been unyielding in his course of action, but boasted in its success (vs. 2).

The issue "is between the use of men for means and means for men."[10] God had purposed that man place his stamp on the uni-

---

[10] John Oman, *Grace and Personality*, p. 237.

verse (Gen. 1:28, 2:19, 20), but the offender reverses the order, dehumanizing even man. A ruler's frustration had swallowed up the inhabitants of Nob, his unrepentant way set for collision course with humanity and heaven.

Christianity must never be less than humanism, the belief that man is somehow the measure of all things. It will wage a ceaseless warfare toward realizing this elusive goal. Every foe of man is an enemy of God, and opposition to God is in the last analysis a threat to man.

PROGRAM

The psalmist adds to his seditious protest the prophecy of overthrow (vs. 5). At a strategic moment, when he is least suspecting, the hero will be taken. The psalmist piles the verbs up as if to indicate the variety of events which will rush together to crush the mighty man. He will be utterly demolished—as one would raze a house (Lev. 14:45); snatched away—like coals picked from the hearth (Isa. 30:14); torn from the security of his home—as if to illustrate the divestment of his pride (Prov. 15:25). The end will be as devastating as it is sudden. There is no repair possible where life and its inherent opportunity have been utterly stifled.

The law of retribution is inviolable. The Talmudic literature pictures Doeg as incapable of perceiving his reflection in the law: "The Holy One, blessed be He, said to the wicked Doeg, 'What hast thou to do to declare (i.e., study) my statutes: when thou comest to the sections dealing with murderers and slanderers, how dost thou expound them?"[11] One is reminded of the boastful words:

> My name is Ozymandias, king of kings:
> Look on my works, ye mighty, and despair!

To which Shelley adds the descriptive account of a shattered monument in a desert waste:

> Nothing beside remains. Round the decay
> Of that colossal wreck, boundless and bare
> The lone and level sands stretch far away.

---

[11]*Sanhedrin* 106b. *The Babylonian Talmud.*

So the text contrasts the prime of man over against his eventual plight (vs. 7); once seemingly unassailable in his power and determination, he has quite succumbed.

It is encouraging to know that the cause of righteousness is assured; but the most difficult question is still unanswered: What are the means by which God will accomplish His victory?

A Spiritual Conflict

"Although we live in the world, we are not carrying on a worldly war, for the weapons of our warfare are not worldly but have divine power to destroy strongholds" (II Cor. 10:3-4). The distinction which is drawn between the sinner and his sin is fundamental and necessary. In his opposition to sin, the Christian hopes to bring the sinner to terms. His conflict is one of concern, not only for those who suffer at the hands of the enemy, but for the enemy himself. The thesis is easily stated but difficult to accept. To strike in love is perhaps more costly to the one who administers the correction than to the one who receives it.

Put another way, the spiritual conflict seeks to preserve rather than to suppress personality. It does not answer death with death but with life. The disciple's purpose is to conserve and construct, not to destroy or eliminate. He must overcome evil with good (Rom. 12:21).

The conflict is spiritual not only in its purpose—to foster life—but in its program—the use of nonmaterial resources and means. Paul spoke of truth, righteousness, gospel, faith, salvation, Spirit, and prayer as characteristic of the warfare (Eph. 6:14-18). One might enlarge on various aspects of the spiritual program, but one illustration, that of prayer, may suffice.

At first observation, prayer seems not only remote from the field of conflict but a candid admission of need. However, we have already observed that reliance on God should be understood in connection with man's assuming his responsible role. It follows that prayer is the divine-human dialogue which enables all available resources to be brought to a given situation.

Spiritual conflict implies not only cooperation between one man and his God, but the militancy of the whole community of faith. Hence, prayer draws redeemed man into battle array. It welds the Christian task force into a fighting unit, making possible the success which escapes the separate endeavors of men.

The combat is spiritual not only in its purpose and program but also in regard to its promise. The encounters do not always, or even with a pattern of increasing frequency, suggest the victory of righteousness. Yet, "we know that even when things are at their worst, the battle is already won. It is won because it is God's battle."[12] The appearance of God in the equation assures triumph (vss. 5-7). Our certainty in this regard is not derived from the proficiency of the Christian soldier or the organization of the military force, but from trust in the Supreme Commander.

A Human Endeavor

Man is never neutral in the universal struggle, but he may be ineffective. Beyond God's provision is the necessary condition of human response: "The rule of God is an order which is outside of us, but it exists only as it is imposed from within."[13] As every soldier knows, there is a psychology of militancy, which involves a necessary transformation from civilian life.

There are at least three aspects of the combatant's response: discipline to obey commands, dedication to the task, and diligent pursual of duties. He is enlisted under the provisions of radical renunciation of his former ties and obedience to orders. He must learn to obey commands, even when the rationale is less than clear, since his view of the battle necessarily lacks the overview of his superior.

The soldier must also be dedicated. That is, he is set apart for the task. Capability may vary according to individuals, but not commitment. As one officer observed: "The Army's order is to go. There is no hint that you must return." It is not surprising that Christ pointed out the importance of weighing the demands of such an undertaking (Luke 14:25-33).

The course of war must be vigorously waged. The idea is not to derive power but to render service, not getting advantage over

---

[12]Archibald Bowman, *The Absurdity of Christianity and Other Essays*, p. 48.

[13]Oman, *op. cit.*, p. 221.

others but giving oneself to them. None served man more faithfully than the Master, and none can minister better than in His sublime name.

A Case for Charity

Love must be embodied, or it will become a justification for indolence. The gift of self without also providing something needed is quite meaningless. Love must "be service done to these needy, weak and miserable human beings, it will be sacrifice, it will be life worn out in daily toil or relinquished at a single blow, in deprivation, humility, weariness, tears and blood, to the likeness of Christ."[14]

Charity is love given concrete form. The expression may vary in terms of its tangibility, from a hearing given to a troubled person to a basket of food presented to a needy family. It may differ in its ultimate value, all the way from the water which momentarily satisfies to that water of life which will keep the man who has drunk of it from ever thirsting again (John 4:13-14). The Biblical concept is to *do* good rather than *be* good (Psa. 34: 14; 37:3, 27; Matt. 5:44; Luke 6:9, 35).

Christ taught His followers to illuminate the world with their good works (Matt. 5:16). These are the concrete means by which the Christian gives himself. Thousands of times over he embodies his love in deeds. Those who are slowest to understand the Christian message thus feel its impact.

A Cause for Struggle

Man is capable of intensifying his evil efforts in the presence of good example, whether reverential faith, responsible behavior, or acts of service. What then? The Christian militant cannot ignore the challenge.

Every society has built into its group life certain restraints meant to benefit the community as a whole. The Christian respects such order, even when it fails to work equitably in many regards (I Pet. 3:14). As a responsible citizen, he plays a role in

---

[14]Jean Mouroux, *The Meaning of Man*, p. 229.

instituting, supporting, and enforcing the regulations, at the same time taking care not to lobby for his peculiar convictions.

The misuse of power need not go unchallenged. Nevertheless, the effect of Christian protest is diminished by at least three snares: the implication that one is speaking for God, the peculiar selectivity of the topics discussed, and the general ineffectiveness of preachments. While the last is self-explanatory, the previous points may be expanded with profit.

Is a holy man automatically better informed concerning social and political decisions? Neither history nor revelation will support that contention. To be sure, the Christian operates under worthy moral principles, but these are seldom easily or categorically applied to social issues. No doubt there are cases where the implications are so clear as to demand protest, but the corrective course of action is more difficult to define. Therefore, the Christian's protest often seems platitudinous and irrelevant.

The priority given to issues is also a point of criticism. The Christian has allowed the shallow to replace the substantial concern. More immediate matters have taken preference over those of long-term significance. Pronouncement has been made on very controversial issues, while there has been hesitancy to offend power structures even when the moral implication was evident.

Protest may take the form of passive resistance, a noncoercive action whereby the person refuses to obey authority, proving to be more or less an obstruction in the process. While it provides a more tangible means of protest, it is effective only in a society amenable to such pressures. In addition, passive resistance has difficulty remaining passive, and even when it does, it may fail by being strong enough only to entrench the opposition.

Coercion is the last possibility. Christ cautioned regarding its use (Matt. 26:52), but employed it under extreme circumstances (John 2:15). Dietrich Bonhoeffer was inclined toward pacifism, by personal disposition and theological leaning, but in the face of brutal Nazi oppression he turned to active resistance. Perhaps the contribution made by such men of action does little more than provide a respite in order that a more excellent way can be found (I Cor. 12:31), but that is no small gift. Time is a precious thing, especially to those who have little of it.

COVENANT

The remaining verses of the psalm may be thought of as a eulogy of the covenant, that which binds man to God in martial purpose (vss. 8-9). They are reflections on the reality which requires struggle, the truth which calls man to active service.

Life in Focus

All things are seen to coalesce in Christ (Col. 1:17). As a result life is not any more simple but is more substantial. There is a universal meaning and perspective which was previously lacking.

On a recent occasion I had the opportunity of viewing several experimental films and afterwards of hearing the producer answer questions on his work. One film especially illustrated the fragmentary nature of meaning, the limited clues to life available. For brief moments living seemed to make some sense, only to become garbled again, to sink into meaningless noises and blurred impressions. Strikingly, the producer professed not even to recognize the catches of meaning I had observed, as though I were better able to understand his experience than was he himself. This may happen in human experience. In any case, Christ pulls life together, enriching the meaning we have experienced and providing that which has been lacking—working episodes into a theme.

With the tenor of life set, the task also falls into place. The Christian's ministry is evangelistic: "Religion can best be understood as referring primarily to that center of ultimate commitment and loyalty from which men derive their understanding of reality, of themselves and their companions, and of what is truly of value."[15]

The Christian's service is encouragement as well as evangelism. His task is to strengthen amenable nature as well as to win commitment to Christ. He must be concerned with the whole man in his most extended situation.

Evangelism, however, is a priority, as Charles McCoy rightly indicates: "Only in a secondary sense and as they tend to represent

---

[15]Charles McCoy, "The Churches and Protest Movements for Racial Justice," *Religion and Social Conflict*, Lee and Marty, eds., p. 38.

limited segments of society, will religious organizations precipitate conflict or offer solutions to situations of tension."[16] The priority of evangelism over encouragement is essentially social rather than personal (Matt. 12:30; Mark 9:40), the priority of the Church as a whole. Within the Christian community, where the individual diversity and calling is expected and respected, each Christian seeks the means for effective witness and articulate testimony.

Logic of the Minority

The Christian army may be mighty, but it is certainly in the minority. The kingdom "appears not in any mass movements, but in those who see on which side true strength lies, and what is mankind's real and abiding gain. . . . it may rule only the loyal few, while over against them still stand the vast organizations of the deluded many."[17] The implications of such a minority status are no doubt many, but we shall limit the discussion to several critical points in regard to the experience itself.

There is a sense in which the Christian is the most undemocratic of men. He rejects the idea that right results from consensus. For this very reason, he is a most valuable addition to the democratic society, for he provides a creative minority to activate and encourage the majority along profitable paths.

The Christian accepts the difficulty in communication which is inherent in a society where there is a marked difference in ideals. Every man interprets events and experience in the light of his particular value structure, and subconsciously evaluates meaning in terms of personal relevance. The process is like a robin gathering twigs and bits of string to make a nest; situations are weighed in the light of personal use. Recognizing this fact, the Christian will not be surprised when communication becomes difficult. He will not categorically dismiss the problem as an indication of human depravity and/or suppose that better clarification will necessarily bring accord. Faith brings one nearer to persons, but often further away from their way of thinking.

[16]*Ibid.*, p. 44.
[17]Oman, *op. cit.*, p. 238.

But what is the Christian to do, since he is part of a minority, about his desire for commendation? From earliest childhood we are directed by positive and negative responses to our acts. We have been more rewarded by a word of appreciation than in a monetary fashion; we have been punished more regularly by silence or words than by physical blows. These cues to action tend to dominate us. The answer is that there are few areas where freedom in Christ is more meaningful than here.

The Christian's liberty in Christ is meant to set him free to serve God in response to his best perception of the divine will. Its practical effect should be to make him appreciative of recognition but not obsessively concerned about gaining it; certainly he will not organize his life around such acclaim. One need only remember the Lord's refusal to accept popular support, and His perseverance in the perceived will of God.

The rationale for the minority may be found in a phrase: "the courage to be free." E. H. Robertson concludes his discussion of this topic with these words: "Each of these stations—discipline, action, suffering, death—requires its own kind of courage for acceptance. It is the courage to be free. . . . It is essential that the various expressions of this courage should be directed towards a purpose, to which God calls."[18] The call of Christ is to the role and logic of a holy minority.

Grace in Abundance

The subject must not be left, however, on a note of austerity and unrewarding discipline. The psalmist compares his experience to the olive tree which is proverbial for its hardiness and fruitfulness (vs. 8). His lot is in sharp contrast to that of his adversary: he prospers rather than being uprooted, is welcomed into the household of God rather than being plucked from his tent, trusts in the mercy of God rather than boasting in wickedness, and abides forever instead of being cut off from the land of the living (cf. vss. 1-5 with vss. 7-8). The optimism of the psalmist suggests that further speculation may be in order.

---

[18]Robertson, *op. cit.*, p. 95.

What is the source and means of gratification for the combatant? The conditions of warfare are seldom superior to those of secure suburbia. However, some deep and lasting friendships are forged in battle. A soldier at the front is forced to ask what is important and who can be trusted. The extremity of the situation is the potential for lasting value. We may suppose that abundance in the Christian's experience does not result from things but from fellowship with both the Almighty and his fellow soldiers of the faith.

It is also true that the worth or importance of the mutual endeavor invests the activity with personal meaning. Following the end of World War II, I underwent, along with many others, a peculiar letdown and increased resentment toward my remaining military obligation. As long as there was an urgent purpose (the end of the war) for our association and service in the military, life made a peculiar kind of sense. But when the purpose had been achieved, the sense of meaning vanished. Much more, the universal and perpetual conflict of good and evil enriches life by the very demands which it makes.

We have said that the Christian life consists not in material possessions but in fellowship (cf. Matt. 4:4), and in the cause which reflects theonomous concern. To this may be added the experience of enablement, the thrill of achievement over what has been a persistent obstacle. The runner who improves his time, the student who masters a difficult equation, and the saint who learns how to turn hostility into creative channels are similarly excited with their new progress. Christian soldiery always confronts us with captivating possibilities. It is the most open-ended challenge ever to confront man. There is always the inviting tomorrow.

CONCLUSION

The Christian is summoned to crusade (Eph. 6:11-18). The arena of conflict is culture, that peculiar creation of man which is a complex of good and evil, of promise and doom. Fashioned out of man's decisions, the legacy of culture reenters as life control, both healing and crippling those who come under its influence.

Neither retreat from nor compromise with culture are viable

options for the believer. His concern is for the will of God, which involves him in service to the whole man. His service begins in the context of the fellowship, where priorities can be faced within the creative interplay of complementary gifts.

There is a peculiar wisdom to the minority which, like Gideon's army, becomes with God a majority. The covenant binds man to God in a task of terrifying proportions but also in a communion of heightened experience, high purpose, and a gratifying sense of achievement.

⟨⟩ *10* ⟨⟩

Retrospect

The past helps clarify for man his nature, prospect, salvation, and responsibility. He cannot escape from history. To ignore it is foolish, to succumb to it is tragic, but to use it as a guide to life is noble. History provides the dynamic dimension for creative living.

Retrospect

1. Praise Yah. Praise the name of Yahweh. Praise, you servants of Yahweh,

2. Who stand in the house of Yahweh, in the courts of the house of our God.

3. Praise Yah, for Yahweh (is) good. Sing psalms to His name, for (He is) gracious;

4. For Yah has chosen Jacob for Himself, Israel for His peculiar treasure;

5. For I know that Yahweh (is) great, and our Lord is above all gods.

6. Everything that pleases Yahweh He did, in the heavens, and in the earth, in the seas and all depths;

7. Who brings up vapors from the end of the earth; who makes lightnings for the rain; who brings the wind out from His storehouses;

8. Who smote the firstborn of Egypt, of man and beast;

9. Who sent signs and wonders into your midst, Egypt, upon Pharaoh and all his servants;

10. Who smote many nations, and slew mighty kings;

11. Sihon, king of the Amorites, and Og, king of Bashan, and all the kingdoms of Canaan,

12. And gave their land for an inheritance, an inheritance to His people Israel.

13. Your name Yahweh (is) for ever; Yahweh, Your remembrance to all generations;

14. For Yahweh will judge His people, and will repent Himself concerning His servants.

15. The idols of the nations (are) silver and gold, the work of men's hands.

16. They have mouths, but will not speak. They have eyes, but will not see.

17. They have ears, but will not hear, nor is there breath in their mouth.

18. Like them are those who make them, (as is) everyone that trusts in them.
19. House of Israel, bless Yahweh! House of Aaron, bless Yahweh!
20. House of Levi, bless Yahweh! You who fear Yahweh, bless Yahweh!
21. Blessed be Yahweh out of Zion, who dwells in Jerusalem! Praise Yah!

PSALM 135

The past is man's legacy. It is the point of his departure, the guide to his direction, and the promise of his potential.

PRELUDE TO HISTORY

Before man developed a historical methodology, and often since, he has spun stories about the past. These tales, or sagas, were meant to fill in the blanks in his recollection, to give substance to dim outlines fading into oblivion. The existence of sagas testifies to man's felt need to link himself to his past but also to his limited capability of doing so. They tell us more of man's psychology than of his history.

Myth may similarly be distinguished from history, but the word has a highly diversified meaning depending on the author who employs it. For instance, myth is roughly synonymous with saga for Barth; it is theological for Bultmann, and both historical and theological for Brunner. Barth dismisses myth as stories of the gods, and he eliminates from this category such events as the resurrection and the creation. Bultmann attempts to retain the theological truth by the process of demythologizing, that is by locating the truth under its antiquated garb. Brunner accepts myth as the necessary manner in which a transcendent God reveals himself to man. There are still other variations in the use of the term, but these suffice to demonstrate the ambiguity involved.

In today's theological discussion, the category of myth seems to add more confusion than clarity. The point we need to keep in mind is that if God is to meet man, it must be where man is— that is, in the making of history. Those who choose to divorce theology from history effectively silence God and make any discussion of religion meaningless.

Man needs history in order to recognize God (vss. 1-5). While credulity leaps in the dark, faith is a response to that for which we have reason. The psalmist speaks of an event—the choice of Israel (vs. 4), and implies a revelation—the knowledge of Yahweh (vs. 5). Here we have a succinct statement, an equation which can be read as *event plus revelation equals history*. Event without revelation would leave God unintelligible still. Revelation without event would have no point of contact with man. God must meet man in history. or else we have no knowledge that such an encounter has occurred.

History is man's avenue not only to God but to knowing himself. Reality is necessarily threatened by man's subjectivity. "It is the objective nature of the historic life which offers the means of drawing modern man out of his increasing sterile subjectivism and back into an inhabitable, if grossly imperfect, world."[1] The explication of man must begin with God, for man is in His image. It must therefore begin with history, for this is the human habitat.

Reflection on history is worship as the psalmist views it. Praise Yahweh, praise His name, praise Him for who He is, praise Him whom you serve, let those who attend Him praise Yahweh, praise Him for His goodness, praise Him for His grace, praise Him for His calling, and praise Him for His greatness (vss. 1-5)!

Worship consists of three things: recalling the ideal believed to have ultimate worth, self-appraisal in the light of that ideal, and rededication to it. Expedient considerations have a way of confusing life's priorities. but history provides the needed perspective to differentiate between the trivial and the trenchant. The psalmist sees the Lord of history and can therefore understand his lot. There is the painful moment of introspection when he senses his failure, followed by the joyful sequel of obedience and blessing.

---

[1]Page Smith, *The Historian and History*, p. 240.

In addition to obedience, "the good or bad will of man manifests itself also in his attitude to God's guidance in history, either thankfully accepting the divine ordinances and praising God, or else resisting and grumbling."[2] God was not pleased with those who complained in the wilderness, and their punishment remains a warning to all who read the record (I Cor. 10:6-11). In contrast, the proverbial sufferer Job could respond: "Naked I came from my mother's womb, and naked shall I return; Yahweh gave, and Yahweh has taken away; blessed be the name of Yahweh" (Job 1:21). Praise is the taste of honey which sweetens the bitter experiences of life.

Historical perspective endows praise with realism. The psalmist knows of God's greatness (vs. 5). "The subject is emphatic in the Hebrew. Whatever the heathens may believe, I can as an Israelite have definite knowledge of God's unique supremacy."[3] History validates worship, and worship elucidates history. Worship of Yahweh is the meaningful prelude to historical reflection.

GROUND OF HISTORY

The psalmist sees the world as created and maintained by God (vss. 6-7). The universe is not eternal or quasi-divine, nor does man exist in the patrimony of the gods, subject to their whims and cunning. Rather, the condition of life consists of divine challenge and human response, a conviction derived from the creation, and sustained by confidence in God's providential activity.

Yahweh is a universal and solicitous sovereign. The psalmist "maintains that not a drop of rain falls from heaven without a divine commission or dispensation to that effect."[4] The existence of evil does not preclude either God's rule or the richness of life as ordered for man's benefit. The sun shines for his warmth. The cool of the night is for his refreshment. The trees yield fruit to satisfy his hunger: St. Francis of Assisi was remarkably sensitive to such matters. "Be Thou praised, my Lord, with all Thy creatures," he rejoiced, "above all Brother Sun, who gives the day and

---

[2]Rudolph Bultmann, *History and Eschatology*, p. 97.
[3]Abraham Cohen, *op. cit.*, p. 441.
[4]Calvin, *Commentary on the Book of Psalms*, V, 176.

lightens us therewith. Be Thou praised, my Lord, of our Sister Mother Earth, which sustains and hath us in rule, and produces divers fruits with coloured flowers and herbs."[5]

Appreciation for the means by which divine care is expressed must not degenerate into nature worship. The distinction between God and the world is clearly defined in creation and perpetuated by His providence. To worship nature would be for man to bow before that which is less than he, and to rob himself of his responsible and creative role.

An Arabic proverb says that a man who turns out other than expected lightens but does not rain. No such contradiction exists between God's reputation and His performance (vs. 7). He is steadfast and dependable, and may be counted upon to terrify the evil and rejoice the heart of the righteous. Humanity lacks such forthright consistency; man's faithlessness stands in bold contrast to God's faithfulness The events of history adequately illustrate man's variance; revelation, however, is necessary to focus events in the light of God's purpose. Both together constitute the nature of the universe. The ground of history is the realization of God's gracious availability, the difference between Creator and creation, and between the resolution of God and the wavering expressions of mankind. Every moment is pregnant with opportunity, the point of encounter between God and man in time.

NATURE OF HISTORY

History is the account of man (vss. 8-12). As Boris Pasternak puts it: "Man does not die in a ditch like a dog; he lives in history."[6] It is not only that which happens to man, but what results from his actions. "*Man makes history* by his responsible (and irresponsible) acts, by how he uses his creative gifts. If he is to be explained solely by nature and biology, then history is unexplained or meaningless because nature, when the free decisions of responsible persons are excluded, is simply a process of change."[7]

[5]Thomas Okey, ed., *The Little Flower of St. Francis*, et. al., p. 295.
[6]Quoted in Smith, *op. cit.*, p. 4.
[7]Aaron Ungersma, *The Search for Meaning*, p. 86.

A delicate balance must be maintained between fate and freedom, between that which determines the course of man's activity
and the alteration of causes in line with personal and social goals.
Otherwise, history and man become inscrutable. The very nature
of the problem is such as to lead one toward an either/or decision,
to determinism or existentialism, to fate or freedom. A third
consideration is therefore desirable—an element which has been
called facticity. By facticity is meant the sum total of determinants in any given situation. It includes not only those environ-
mental factors external to man, but the physical and psychological
makeup of the person. Facticity rescues freedom from fate, and
fate from freedom.

The point can be illustrated from the text of the psalm. The
psalm has been described as a mosaic, a work constructed out of
bits and pieces of other works. For instance, verse 1 is perhaps
indebted to Psalm 113:1, verse 2 to Psalm 134:1, verse 4 to Deu-
teronomy 7:6, verse 7 to Jeremiah 10:13, verses 10-12 to Psalm
136:17-22, and the remainder of the psalm to Isaiah 44:12-20,
Jeremiah 6:10, and Psalm 115:4-11. Nonetheless, the psalm has a
clearly liturgical setting which demonstrates that the author used
his sources to produce a new work for the purpose of worship.
The dependence exhibited in the text became the occasion for a
creative production.

Facticity also saves fate from freedom. "Praise and blame are
as meaningless apart from continuity of character as they are
meaningless apart from some kind of freedom."[8] Complete inde-
terminism would frustrate history and rectitude as quickly as
would a thoroughgoing determinism. The psalmist identifies himself with the devout lineage of Israel, assuming the legacy of faith
and continuity of perspective.

History concerns man, but it is inevitably an interpretation of
man's experience. Viewing the assassination of Julius Caesar apart
from the institutional conflict which gave rise to it sheds little
light on the incident itself. Any event or series of events may be
interpreted within larger circumferences of meaning, as illustrated
in the psalmist's equation: event plus revelation equals history.

---

[8]David Elton Trueblood, *Philosophy of Religion*, p. 283.

History is progressive. It is going somewhere, and the place it is going is not just anywhere. God's purpose with the world is in the process of being achieved. Man builds with God's purpose or he is broken by it. Augustine gave this view classical expression: "This race we have distributed into two parts, the one consisting of those who live according to man, the other of those who live according to God. And these we also mystically call the two cities, or the two communities of men, of which the one is predestined to reign eternally with God, and the other to suffer eternal punishment with the devil."[9]

This is not to suggest an undue optimism, as if God's purpose will be reached apart from His climactic assault on the kingdoms of this world; but neither should it rule out God's working in history. As Arnold Toynbee astutely observes: "While civilizations rise and fall and, in falling, give rise to others, some purposeful enterprise, higher than theirs, may all the time be making headway, and, in a divine plan, the learning that comes through the suffering caused by the failures of civilizations may be the sovereign means of progress."[10] In similar fashion the psalmist interprets the fall of those who oppressed Israel (vss. 8-9) and resisted their march (vss. 10-11), as well as the reception of the land as an inheritance (vs. 12).

History is progressive but not perpetual. It has a *telos*, a fulfillment, a date with divine destiny. Christ is the climax of history. He is the fullness of the divine revelation, the very nature of the Holy One taken flesh. In His life, death, and resurrection we have the most complete investment of event with revelation. This means that we can see history in its truest meaning through the advent of Christ. The consummation of history awaits the future, but that future will be with the same Jesus.

DYNAMICS OF HISTORY

History is about man as he is seen in the light of God's unchanging person and unvarying purpose (vss. 13-14). We must

---

[9] Aurelius Augustine, *The City of God*, II, p. 49.

[10] Arnold Toynbee, *Civilization on Trial* and *The World and the West*, p. 25.

now consider the dynamics of history, the means by which man learns to structure his experience in order to make use of the divine opportunity. Two illustrations will provide the necessary guidelines.

Augustine pondered the promise and provision of God which resulted in the deliverance from Egypt (cf. vss. 8-9): "Moses, being stealthily kept from the murders of the infants, was brought to the royal house, God preparing to do great things by him . . . and became so great a man that he—yea, rather God, who had promised this to Abraham, by him—drew that nation, so wonderfully multiplied, out of the yoke of hardest and most grievous servitude."[11] While the deliverance itself was the prominent event to be recited to each succeeding generation (Exod. 12:26-27), Augustine was impressed by the relation of the incident to the foregoing pledge of God, and by the fact that Yahweh was preparing a deliverer before the lords of Egypt had conspired to oppress the Hebrews. While events were breaking around God's people with terrifying suddenness, He had already provided the means of resolution.

Josephus turned his attention to the service rendered by Moses as a true servant of God: "I would demonstrate that Moses did not fail in any one thing that he foretold them; and because it is for the good of mankind, and that they may learn this caution—not to say anything that may displease God, lest he be provoked to wrath."[12] The expediency of Pharaoh is in contrast to the persisting wisdom of Moses in each circumstanc of life.

The lessons are clear, but what is the dynamic at work? History first answers the question: "Who am I?" "Having been is also a kind of being—perhaps the surest kind. . . . Though past, these possibilities are now safely ensconced in the past for all eternity and time can no longer change them."[13] The individual is too changeable, his society too uncertain, for one to ignore the assistance of history in drawing his experience into focus.

History also offers a key to answering the query: "What might

[11]Augustine, *The City of God*, II, p. 162.
[12]Flavius Josephus, "Antiquities of the Jews," *The Works of Flavius Josephus*, Henry Stebbing, ed., pp. 81-2.
[13]Viktor Frankl, *The Doctor and the Soul*, p. 38.

I be?" "Knowing yourself means knowing what you can do, and since nobody knows what he can do until he tries, the only clue to what man can do is what man has done. The value of history, then, is that it teaches us what man has done and thus what man is."[14] The point is well taken. Man is his potential. From the past he may determine the heights to which he may climb, and the dismal depths to which he may sink.

The varying fortunes of man (vss. 8-12) are in sharp contrast to the persisting offer of God (vss. 13-14). History is the answer to the inquiry: "To whom can I turn for assistance?" The steadfastness of God is life's stability. More certain than the natural laws we take for granted is the moral law we try to ignore (Gal. 6:7). History tells us of folly and faith.

We need only recall the analogous situation of a child to his parents to sense the importance of having a supportive and consistent environment. As the child benefits from an encouraging and unaltering parental pattern, so man finds God's moral law a blessing.

History ultimately speaks to the concern: "What ought I to do?" The precedents are not always easy to interpret and are still more difficult to apply. Offenses must come, but the righteous man is encouraged to know that, while judged for his wrong, God will not abandon him to destruction (vs. 14). History tells man of judgment tempered with grace.

The past helps clarify for man his nature, prospect, salvation, and responsibility. He cannot escape from history. To ignore it is foolish, to succumb to it is tragic, but to use it as a guide to life is noble. History provides the dynamic dimension for creative living.

SEARCH FOR HISTORY

The psalmist resumes the theme of the false gods in verses 15-18. They have mouths which do not speak, ears that cannot hear, and eyes that do not see. They create nothing but are created. The praise of man cannot breathe life into them, and his worship links him in their death.

---

[14]Robin Collingwood, *The Idea of History*, p. 10.

It was a religious world to which the psalmist addressed himself. The gods were numerous, often acting as patrons to the nations, but always to be considered and placated. Epics were written to extol them—as for instance the *Enuma Elish* and the Babylonian favorite Marduk. History fared poorly in such a context; event was distorted by the precocious acts of the divinities. Man's initiative could hardly be distinguished from the skill he had developed to manipulate the deities.

History requires man to be responsible; "it is incumbent upon him through his remembrance of the past to carve out a new path for himself."[15] The death of the gods was an invitation to event and the history which depended upon it.

Our age has rapidly depopulated the realm of the gods, threatening them with extinction, but history is still endangered. We recall the equation: event plus revelation equals history. Will Herberg warns us that "the definition of life in terms of the 'sacred history' of God's dealings with men . . . is the only alternative to the idolatrous 'totalization' of one or another of the partial histories which make up our lives."[16] To attempt to understand even apart from revelation is to interpret a dialogue as a monologue, an encounter as a personal reflection, and an end as a means.

The forces of reduction threaten to obliterate history. Meaning becomes practically limited to empirical observation, and physical law is expressed in mathematical equation. History becomes sociology—man given over to the control of his conditions. Anthropology becomes biology—man demoted to being the child of geographic and economic conditions. The result is strikingly similar to antiquity's view of man—the challenge-response ideal is lost and man is again object rather than subject, the servant instead of the master of means. Modern man's death is as final as those who worship the lifeless gods of the ancients (vs. 18).

POSTSCRIPT TO HISTORY

The psalmist concludes his mosaic as he began it—with praise (vss. 19-21). The liturgical cycle is complete—Yahweh is exalted

---

[15]Karl Jaspers, *Man in the Modern Age*, p. 215.
[16]Will Herberg, "Biblical Faith as Heilsgeschichte," p. 29.

as the Lord of history. He has blessed the houses of Israel, Aaron, and Levi; He hears those who fear Him, irrespective of lineage (vss. 19-20).

Faith needs history: "Without proper appropriation of faith's heritage man suffers from a rootless religion. Faith must be firmly rooted."[17] This fact was strikingly illustrated in the nineteenth-century effort to distinguish between Jesus of history and the Christ of faith. Each writer produced his own scheme for getting behind the New Testament records, but it remained for Albert Schweitzer to demonstrate the extreme subjectivity reflected in these attempts, and their failure to present anything more than the preference of the author in reconstructing a Jesus-legend.[18]

The failure was followed with a preoccupation with the Christ of faith. The Christ-idea replaced the historic figure. Some theologians stood against the trend, but their numbers were few and their voices generally not strong. The pendulum has swung again, and of necessity, for faith needs history. Joachim Jeremias summarizes the need: "We *must* continually return to the historical Jesus and his message. The sources demand it; the kerygma, which refers us back from itself, also demands it. To put it in theological terms, the Incarnation implies that the story of Jesus is not only a possible subject for historical research, study, and criticism, but demands all of these."[19]

Not only does faith need history, but history needs faith. The psalmist speaks less of history in general than in the particular of God's assured working with His people (vss. 19-21). Israel was a despised and oppressed people, but God had raised them up. They had no land, but Yahweh fulfilled His promise to give them a prosperous property. They lacked leadership but God raised it up. They had no future, but were given an inheritance in which all nations would be blessed. History was practically the self-authentication of God to the community of faith.

Faith without history is credulity, but history without faith is blind. The meaning of every event of critical significance is con-

---

[17]Nels F. S. Ferré, *The Finality of Faith*, p. 23.
[18]Albert Schweitzer, *The Quest for the Historical Jesus*.
[19]Joachim Jeremias, *The Problem of the Historical Jesus*, pp. 14-15.

troversial. Even the resurrection of Christ from the day of its
occurrence was given an alternative explanation (Matt. 28:12-15).
Faith is not selective, choosing what it wishes to see, but respon-
sive, accepting the divine challenge as it is revealed. So the call of
Christ to Martin Luther meant that he must leave the monastery,
and accept blame and persecution in order to serve his generation.

History is testimonial. It deals with concrete events rather than
ambiguous speculation. For Israel, "the Exodus from Egypt,
which they were convinced was a sheer miracle of deliverance,
was the central symbol. Far from having recourse to arguments
such as the Greek thinkers encouraged, the Israelites would have
considered such arguments abstract or even tiresome."[20] Similarly,
the apostles bore witness to the resurrection and subsequent
ministries of the Lord. History is both the record of God's faithfulness and the invitation to a similar rewarding experience.

History is dynamic, involving the progressive movement toward a climactic conclusion; each step of the way is an opportunity for man to more fully realize his place in the divine purpose. It is dynamic because it allows man to entertain profitably
the questions pertaining to his being, prospect, support, and responsibility. It is dynamic because it preserves the challenge-
response ideal, escaping from both the patrimony of the gods and
the reductionism of the secular. History is alive due to God's
presence, and to the degree to which man is aware of himself and
his opportunity.

There have always been signs of decay in civilization. The
West seems to reflect many such indications along with some
signs of resurgent strength. Christianity has long been identified
with Western civilization, contributing much to it and benefiting
not a little in return. What if the West succumbs to pressure from
without and/or cancer from within? What is the future for
Christian faith? Toynbee's answer is provocative: "If our secular
Western civilization perishes, Christianity may be expected not
only to endure but to grow in wisdom and stature as the result of
a fresh experience of secular catastrophe."[21] He recalls how

---

[20]Trueblood, *op. cit.*, p. 133.
[21]Toynbee, *op. cit.*, p. 209.

Christianity not only survived the collapse but became heir to the Roman Empire. No exacting parallel is possible or asked for. The point is that faith is not in the past, but in the God who was revealed there (vss. 19-21). The vessels which held something of God's blessing were not in themselves durable. Time has a way of exploiting human defection to its destructiveness, but God does not perish in the conflagration.

History has fulfilled its task when it has brought man to face the present. Thus, the psalmist urges man to praise God, to lift holy hands and joyous voices to His acclaim. The past is prelude. The present is possibility, but the potential of the present is in the past. Without the past, man is defenseless against his enemies, certainly against the very nausea of dull routine itself.

Man's need for the past is no less evident in the sagas of antiquity than in the reductionism of contemporary thought. The persisting clue to history is the interpretation of event in the light of God's revelation, the record of divine challenge and human response. When man has seen the potential of the present, the past has achieved its pedagogical purpose.

11

Prospect

. . . *the* status quo *cannot be idolized. God has not been
captured by any institution or any means of operation.
Nor is the new to be embraced because of its novelty—
change has no inherent benefit. Hope, however, does
have "the power of making things fluid." It is the
catalyst which makes divine ferment possible, the incentive toward unrealized perfection.*

Prospect

To the choir director. With stringed instruments.
A psalm. A song.

1. God be merciful to us and bless us, (and) make His face shine upon us,

2. That Your way be known upon earth, Your deliverance among all nations.

3. Let the people praise You, God, let all the people praise You.

4. Let the nations rejoice and sing for joy, because You shall judge the people righteously, and guide the nations upon earth. Selah.

5. Let the people praise You, God; let all the people praise You.

6. The earth has yielded its increase, and God, our God, has blessed us.

7. God has blessed us; let all the ends of the earth reverence Him.

PSALM 67 *Sun*
bul/.

There is no today without tomorrow. Viktor Frankl reached this conclusion as a result of pondering survival in the concentration camp: "The prisoner who had lost faith in the future—his future—was doomed. With his loss of belief in the future, he also lost his spiritual hold; he let himself decline and become subject to mental and physical decay."[1] *Similarly, the exceptionally high casualty rate among American prisoners of war during the Korean conflict was not for the most part caused by physical abuse, but by psychological disintegration. These are extreme situations, but they illustrate a phenomenon so obvious that we habitually discount it. Man's health requires hope. He is probably the only terrestrial being for whom this is true. His nature dictates the condition of survival. Time for him is not a series of unrelated incidents but a course toward a little-perceived future. Without hope he is less than a beast—a malfunctioning organism.*

PENULTIMATE AND HOPE

The psalmist beautifully captures man's aspiration in three petitions, each concluding with an exhortation to praise (vss. 1-3, 4-5, 6-7). He reflects the fulfillment without which life proves to be a failure. His prospect provides the purpose for man's existence.

The occasion for the psalm is the harvest. Among agricultural people harvest time is the summons to celebration. The threat of the long winter is dismissed by a full larder. In this psalm we have the situation and the spiritual significance given to the event —the world and the Word (vss. 1-3).

It is significant that hope tends to precede and transcend the objects to which it seems attached. For instance, at a relatively unguarded moment you may discover an anticipation that you cannot yet define in terms of a given object. In other words hope may exist without conscious awareness of a desirable object. Furthermore, the very things which we hope and think will satisfy,

---

[1] *Man's Search For Meaning*, p. 74.

fail to do so. That is, hope transcends the objects to which we relate it by our application. To say it still another way, hope is *more* and may be *other* than a desire for the factors generally assumed to explain its existence.

Hope ties man to eternity. It may be a cruel self-deception, or it may reflect a reality of the most profound nature. C. S. Lewis suggests three ways for explaining this phenomenon of human experience: the way of the fool, the way of the disillusioned, and the way of the Christian.[2]

1. *The way of the fool.* The fool blames circumstances for his failure to achieve. If he had married another, if the marriage had been sanctified by a church wedding, if he had not married so early in life, if they had not lived in such close proximity to her parents, there would have been success. However, no matter how he may alter things, the fool is still plagued by lack of fulfillment.

2. *The way of the disillusioned.* The disillusioned man attributes hope to the idealism of youth, something to be put away when one becomes a man. Life does not reward his aspirations, and he must make the best of it. Be realistic. Be hard. Let common sense stifle those immature sensibilities. The disillusioned guards himself against the awareness of hope, fearful that it is a sign of weakness, oblivious that to many it has been the source of strength.

3. *The way of the Christian.* The Christian is not alone in his conviction that there are satisfactions which correspond to the desires which exist. If a duckling wishes to swim, there is such a thing as water. If there is the felt need of sex, there is sexual experience. If there is an aspiration which tends to precede and transcend earthly experience, the probability is that some aspect of it corresponds to the world beyond. Perhaps earthly pleasures were not meant to satisfy hope but to stimulate it toward a future realization.

Hope belongs to what Dietrich Bonhoeffer calls the *penultimate*, literally the things before the last. He means by this all that precedes faith in Christ, everything which is implied in being a natural man. Jesus is the fulfillment of life, the Omega beyond

---

[2]Lewis, *Mere Christianity*, pp. 117-118.

which life does not go. He is the ultimate. But hope is not a
condition peculiar to the experience of Christ. Hope belongs to
man, and manhood is antecedent to justification.[3]

Hope accepts trial. The long hours of tilling the soil, sowing
the seed, cultivating the produce, and reaping the fruit are compounded by the variables of weather and the caprice of men.
Hope employs these factors as part of a creative process of living,
and can rejoice with the good harvest or retrench for a sustained
testing. Hope is the ingredient which makes life possible, without
which even prosperity is empty and threatening.

Hope exists alongside the potential for despair. "The truth is
that there can strictly speaking be no hope except when the
temptation to despair exists."[4] Human experience knows no un-
disturbed serenity which does not smack of escapism. The very
intensity of the harvest celebration testifies to the persisting fears
which had hounded the enterprise.

The penultimate consists of humanity: its trial, despair, and
hope. It also includes responsibility, the need to contribute according to one's capability. Society has a reciprocal obligation
to the handicapped but none for the parasite. The nature of responsibility requires repeated definition, but its existence is the
datum of life, the assumption without which man slips into moral
nihilism.

While the content of the penultimate is humanity, its context is
temporality (Psa. 103:15-16). Hope also is transitory. It perishes
with man unless it finds fulfillment beyond him. Hope is the smile
of eternity, awaiting man's recognition.

We have seen that the psalm reflects not only the situation—the
incident of the penultimate—but a spiritual significance, an
anticipation of the ultimate, or reconciliation in Christ. What is
the relationship of the penultimate and ultimate? Bonhoeffer suggests two unfavorable resolutions:

1. *Radicalism*. The radical solution breaks sharply with the
penultimate, fostering an extreme hostility between Christ and the
world. All must go into the judgment. The world reminds the

---

[3]Bonhoeffer, *Ethics*, pp. 133ff.
[4]Gabriel Marcel, *Homo Viator*, p. 36.

Christian of its perishing nature; the law hangs like a poised sword over man's head.

(2.) *Compromise.* The compromise alternative is quite the reverse. There is naïve acceptance of the world as it is; the voice of judgment is lost. The penultimate stands in its own right without fear of the ultimate.

Bonhoeffer rejects both: "Radicalism hates time, and compromise hates eternity. Radicalism hates patience, and compromise hates decision. Radicalism hates wisdom, and compromise hates simplicity. Radicalism hates moderation and measure, and compromise hates the immeasurable. Radicalism hates the real, and compromise the word."[5]

What, then, is the solution? Bonhoeffer finds the answer in the incarnate, crucified, and risen Christ. An ethic based upon the cross and resurrection alone would lead to radicalism, and one based solely on the incarnation, to compromise. In that Christ was crucified, God has pronounced judgment on the world, and in that He was raised, God has imparted new life. Because Christ was incarnate the believer can and must live the man.

Practically, this thesis means that man lives in the penultimate by the power of the ultimate. He participates most fully in the human experience because of the perspective and power of the resurrected Christ. "Christian life means being a man through the efficacy of the incarnation; it means being sentenced and pardoned through the efficacy of the cross; and it means living a new life through the efficacy of the resurrection."[6]

What does hope mean when it has embraced the Christ? It is not *terminus* but *thither*—it does not come to an end but points to a future. The psalmist prays that God's *way* may be known (vs. 2). If faith had achieved its destination, it would no longer be necessary, for sight would replace it. Hope is similarly transitory for the believer. It is a journey, and as such offers the opportunity of relating the fragmented pieces of life to the final destination. It saves man from momentary expediency and delivers him to a sustained course of action.

[5] Dietrich Bonhoeffer, *Ethics*, p. 130.
[6] *Ibid.*, pp. 132-133.

Hope is also confidence and priority: "Once a man has found God in his earthly bliss and has thanked him for it, there will be plenty of opportunities for him to remind himself that these earthly pleasures are only transitory, and that it is good for him to accustom himself to the idea of eternity."[7] Similarly, the psalmist could rejoice in God's benefits and pray for His deliverance (vs. 2). The believer walks the way in confidence, and with a sensitivity toward things of import.

PROMISE OF HOPE

While the first petition hinted at transcending the penultimate, the second warns of its destruction (vss. 4-5), anticipating a benevolent and righteous judgment. The promise of equity should be enough to cause the nations to rejoice and burst forth into song.

The penultimate is terminated by death, and death ends in the judgment (I Cor. 15:24-26). Paul calls death man's last enemy. It is a concern which presses for consideration, and it is doubtful that any thinking man can be oblivious to the question of his destiny or fully accept the fact that he will die.

Death strips man of his presumption, checking his unreasoning accumulation of material things (Luke 12:20). Death is raw. It cruelly strips man of his sophistication, numbs his once-critical mind, incapacitates his limbs, and decays his cherished features. It is perhaps this starkness which causes man to pause and deliberate on the meaning of existence: "Death, personal death, forces us to ask ultimate questions."[8]

If death is the inescapable question mark raised over life, the nature of judgment is given us in the psalmist's reply (vs. 4). He tells us three things concerning the judgment: God will remember man, assess his situation with equity, and will guide the nations in a solicitous fashion. Death appears to be the final episode in man's brief career, but the word tells us that we are mistaken in

---

[7]Bonhoeffer, *Letters and Papers from Prison*, p. 57.

[8]James Schall, "The Social Mission of Christianity," *Current Trends in Theology*, Wolf and Schall, eds., p. 213.

this regard. After death is the judgment (Heb. 9:27). Man is not forgotten, allowed to waste into oblivion. Life has a date with destiny.

The thought of justice is a conciliatory note, reflecting the posture of the psalmist (cf. vs. 2). The man who has faced his sin with God need not fear the sentence of judgment. To choose the world in preference to God will mean the loss of both eternal and abundant life, but to claim God rather than the world is to gain both. The fool tries to retain the penultimate, but this terminates in death. The wise man can rejoice in the recompense of God, the legacy of the ultimate.

A further word of comfort is expressed in verse 4: "The verb is used of God guiding Israel through the wilderness to the land of promise; the same guidance is at the disposal of all peoples if, like Israel, they accept Him as their God."[9] The thought involves, in addition to instruction, the sustenance and protection of the Almighty. The offer is enlarged to include all men and intensified as if to erase even the foreboding of death.

The promise of hope is the pledge of God. It is not simply a wish but God's way. Jesus could assure the bereaved: "I am the resurrection and the life. He that believes in me, though he were dead, yet shall he live, and whoever lives and believes in me shall never die' (John 11:25-26). Hope is faith in Christ cast into the future. Paul describes Christian hope in various ways. It is "the hope of the gospel," the reality of the good news (Col. 1:23). It is "the hope of salvation," the final deliverance of the believer from the arena of sin (I Thess. 5:8). It is "the hope of righteousness," the conformity of the believer to the will of God (Gal. 5:5). It is the "hope . . . of the glory of . . . God," the participation with God in His reign and magnificence (Titus 2:13, cf. Rom. 5:2). It is the "hope of eternal life," the full realization of the life already in the believer's possession (Titus 1:2). It is "the hope of his calling," the prospect of those who are beneficiaries of Christ's invitation (Eph. 1:18).

It is clear from the above references that the ultimate has both a beginning and an end—a conception and a consummation. Paul

---

[9]Cohen, *op. cit.,* p. 208.

had experienced the results of faith, but he awaited the prospects of hope. Hope aspires to a heaven where the contract of faith will be realized. Hope also knows of a hell, the conclusion to failed opportunity. Hell is not an extension of the penultimate but the memory of it. The penultimate is preparation for Christ, but hell is His absence. There is no place in heaven or hell for hope, because hope is a quality of man in time. Hope has fulfilled its purpose when it has led man to choose his eternal future wisely.

PRACTICE OF HOPE

The final petition of Psalm 67 takes an intensely practical turn (vss. 6-7). Ray Petry has observed that "an age such as ours is accustomed to the preservation of a token eschatology concurrent with a practicing repudiation of it."[10] An accent on hope is not equivalent to living by its code, for expectation is meant to have a purifying effect: "Denying ungodliness and worldly lusts, we should live soberly, righteously, and godly, in this present world; looking for that blessed hope, and the glorious appearing of the great God and our Saviour Jesus Christ" (Titus 2:12-13, KJV). Peter joined Paul's concern with the admonition: "Seeing then that all these things shall be dissolved, what manner of persons ought ye to be in all holy conversation and godliness, looking for and hasting unto the coming of the day of God" (II Peter 3:11-12, KJV).

A concern for the future which does not focus on the present is a false hope. Fear of conditions may cause man to flee to the past or future, but reverence of God brings him to the present. There are few more useless things than speculating on the details of prophecy, or more profitable than the implication of eschatology for ethics.

The first role which hope plays is to keep the penultimate from becoming ultimate: "Christianity in theory frees the political and practical order from the perennial threat of itself becoming a religion, for it establishes that this life and its proper tasks are important but temporal."[11] Hope knows that no human institution

---

[10] Ray C. Petry, *Christian Eschatology and Social Thought*, p. 371.
[11] Schall, *op. cit.*, p. 218.

perfectly embodies the divine prerogatives. Democracy does not, and neither does the Church. There must always be the flexibility for one to obey God rather than man, even when in so doing he may be deceiving himself. The right of dissent must be zealously guarded. There is an inevitable tension between the world and the Word, a tension which hope seeks to perpetuate.

Hope realizes that there is a margin of error in theology, just as in any other science. It reminds the cleric that he may speak for God but that he is not God. Like any other specialist, he is prone to pontificate, and hope suggests a modicum of humility coupled with some humor. It helps the real Deity stand out.

It follows that the *status quo* cannot be idolized. God has not been captured by any institution or any means of operation. Nor is the new to be embraced because of its novelty—change has no inherent benefit. Hope, however, does have "the power of making things fluid."[12] It is the catalyst which makes divine ferment possible, the incentive toward unrealized perfection. Hope also gives man honesty, disavowing the extragavance of his claims.

The second service which hope renders is to assist the penultimate to function as the penultimate, to prepare the way for Christ. The means by which the penultimate achieves its purpose would seem to be charity, equity, and dialogue. Life is never void of need or of the necessity to satisfy it. Christ did not turn away the hungry multitude or turn His back on any request. The disciple assumes his Master's posture: "It is for the love of Christ . . . that I share my bread with him and that I share my dwelling with the homeless. If the hungry man does not attain to faith, then the guilt falls on those who refused him bread. To provide the hungry man with bread is to prepare the way for the coming of grace."[13]

Charity must be coupled with equity. It is not enough to do for another, but each one must be enabled to do for himself. The rights of man must be achieved and maintained, as Calvin interprets the prohibition against stealing: "The purport is, that injustice being an abomination to God, we must render to every man

---

[12]Marcel, *op. cit.*, p. 41.
[13]Bonhoeffer, *Ethics*, p. 137.

his due."[14] The reformer's elaboration suggests that this involves not coveting that which is another's, protecting that which is one's own, and endeavoring to guarantee the property of others against encroachment. Charity without equity provides a temporary adjustment but no long-range solution. Equity apart from charity fails to consider the imperfections of man and society.

Dialogue must be added to charity and equity to round out this ideal of the penultimate. Being is formed through dialogue, and society cannot long survive without it. Dialogue is the means of inculcating learning, ascertaining truth, and expressing relationship. It is especially critical to the preparation for Christ: "The most important thing about this dialogue between the Church and the world is that God acts in and through it to influence both the Church and the world and to judge, purify, and transform both."[15] Dialogue keeps open the creative possibility of society: it keeps the eye to God's action, the ear to God's word, and the voice to clarify God's intention. Hope ministers in the name of Christ to the needs, rights, and creative possibilities of the penultimate, assisting it in preparation for the Lord.

The third task which hope undertakes is witness to the ultimate, through circumspection and compassion. The early Church saw the need of a way of life which would reflect the principles of God amid the plight of the pagan. "It is good therefore that he who has learned the ordinances of the Lord as many as have been written should walk in them. For he who does these things shall be glorified in the kingdom of God, and he who chooses the others shall perish with his works."[16] In calling the believer out of the world, hope testifies to the nature of the word, and invites man to the Way.

While circumspection calls man away from sin, compassion draws him to service. Hope is not monasticism but ministry. Christ's concern touched a condemned adulteress, a partisan Samaritan, a self-righteous religious leader, a contagious leper, and a dishonest tax collector. His sympathy led Him to the outcasts

---

[14] Calvin, *Institutes of the Christian Religion*, II, 8, 46.
[15] Reuel Howe, *The Miracle of Dialogue*, p. 15.
[16] *Epistle of Barnabas*, XXI.

of society and earned Him the reputation of being their companion. The disciple is constrained at the thought of such love to depart from self-seeking to serve others (II Cor. 5:14-15). Hope testifies to two circles—one of the circumscription of God's will and the other the extent of God's love.

Hope introduces man to the present. It resists the penultimate's effort to become the ultimate, assists the penultimate in achieving its destined role, and confesses the ultimate. Hope reaches into the future for guidelines for the present. It is practical or it is not hope.

PRAISE OF HOPE

As has been noted, all three of the psalmist's petitions terminate in an expression of praise (vss. 3, 5, 7). Hope's distinctive attitude is a eulogy of spirit. No doubt we have tended to limit our emotions to influences from the past and present, and failed to appreciate how they are crystallized in terms of future expectation. The text corrects us in this regard.

J. B. Phillips tells of a group of young people who did not understand his reference to worship. He explained it to them as "three cheers for God." Writing to a later audience, Phillips attempted to trace the desire to praise along two main lines: creation and incarnation.[17] One can hardly help but be impressed by any work of excellence and the world is full of excellent works. Phillips caught himself musing: "I would like to meet the architect of this or that." He found himself tracing all those things which made him wonder, love, and admire, to their Source, to the Creator. Similarly, the psalmist acknowledges the means through which God has blessed the people (vs. 7).

Praise results from the God who not only made man but who became man. In creation we see His capacity, but in the incarnation we witness His compassion. God is a Christlike being, one who stands with man. The Word, more than the world, cultivates our worship. Each footfall of Christ is echoed by our acclaim of God.

---

[17] J. B. Phillips, *Plain Christianity*, pp. 60-61.

Hope is not unrealistic; it is the discernment of a deeper reality. It does not deny the vicissitudes of life, but lays hold of a steady hand which guides us through them. Hope does not reduce the ingredients of living but adds God to the equation. Hope shouts, not because there is no enemy, but because God gives the triumph. Hope sings, not because there is no night, but because God gives songs in the night. The pulse of hope is praise.

PRÉCIS

Man is future-oriented. He is not simply driven by internal and external forces, but drawn by his aspirations. His very survival depends upon a proper estimate of this facet of his experience.

Hope both attends and transcends life. It tends to precede and not to be exhausted by the things for which we rationalize its presence. Hope exists in but points beyond the penultimate. It defines the way, suggests the confidence, and describes the priority of the ultimate. Hope is the datum of life, the tension with death, and the tale of judgment. It defies the prospect that meaning might be swallowed up in death. It responds to a voice which beckons man to take God's way and experience His redemption.

Man lives in the present. Hope provides him with the means to do so. It resists the effort of the penultimate to become the ultimate, the human institution to replace Christ's call. It assists the penultimate in fulfilling its rightful service through acts of charity, performance of equity, and exercise of dialogue. It completes its threefold ministry by testimony to the ultimate—a combination of circumspection and compassion, a call both away from and to the world.

Hope is not blind because it lacks sight. Rather, it sees through the eyes of God and rejoices in His beneficent intent. The future is captured for the present. Anxiety is replaced by acclaim. Creation takes on a pristine purity, and the incarnation is pregnant with personal significance. Praise acknowledges the divine Person, and reverence accepts His purpose (vs. 7).

⊶ *12* ⊷

Panorama

*Ethics, then, is situational, if we mean by this that de-
cisions must at least in part reflect the unique character
of the given circumstances. There are no pat answers,
no godly gimmicks, no simple directions. Life is complex, and faith faces out on life.*

Panorama

*To the choir director.   Not to be suppressed.
A psalm of Asaph.   A song.*

1. We give thanks to you, God, we give thanks. Your name being near, we number Your wondrous deeds.
2. At a time I appoint will I judge with equity.
3. When the earth and all its inhabitants are dissolved, I will form its pillars. Selah.
4. I said to the boastful: "Do not boast," and to the wicked: "Do not raise your horn."
5. "Do not raise your horn on high. Do not speak with an unbent neck;
6. "For exaltation does not come from the east or the west or from the wilderness;
7. "Because God judges, putting down the one and raising the other;
8. "For in the hand of Yahweh is a cup with fermented wine fully mixed, and He will pour out of this, and all the wicked of the earth will drain it to the dregs."
9. But I will declare forever. I will sing praises to the God of Jacob.
10. And all the horns of the wicked He will cut off, (and) the horns of the righteous will be exalted.

PSALM 75

In the Christian life the accent is on the present. This is true whether the reference is to the past (I Cor. 10:6), or to the future (II Peter 3:11). All that has been exists for the present; all that may be depends upon the present. It is appropriate that our concluding discussion focuses on that moment of opportunity between what has been and what will be.

I–YOU

Man suffers from monotony, a wearisomeness bordering on disgust. Sartre calls it nausea, a loathing to the point of sickness. It is the sign of losing subjectivity, the incapability of structuring life in terms of personal goals.

Tedium is the clue to subhumanity. It warns us of man's propensity to live out his life on the animal level of existence. Consequently, Jaspers can call anxiety a good thing: "Anxiety is to be approved. It is a reason for hope."[1] Anxiety at least suggests an awareness of self as subject. Similarly, Sartre defends his existentialism as humanism: "We can begin by saying that existentialism, in our sense of the word, is a doctrine that does render human life possible, a doctrine also, which affirms that every truth and every action imply both an environment and a human subjectivity."[2]

The daily routine of life, especially when compounded by a technological society, tends to dehumanize. The machine readily becomes the model for man. A person tends to be identified by the service he renders rather than by being a unique person. He wears out, not from overuse, but from psychological friction over his distasteful role. Death is sometimes preferred to this sort of existence.

There are other more subtle means of coping with the unpleasant, such as the use of drugs or an uncritical obedience to a cause. It takes courage to *be*, to accept not only the determinants of one's circumstance but the possibility of modifying the situation so as to allow still greater freedom. But this is what it means to be

---

[1] Karl Jaspers, *The Origin and Goal of History*, p. 150.
[2] Jean-Paul Sartre, "Existentialism is a Humanism," *Existentialism from Dostoevsky to Sartre*, Kaufman, ed., p. 288.

a person, a subject among other selves. This is what distinguishes the I-You relationship from an "it." The former are living and acting, while the latter is lifeless and acted upon.

I–YOU–THOU

To the situation and self the psalmist adds a critical third factor —God (vs. 1). Bonhoeffer observed that "responsibility is a total response of the whole man to the whole of reality."[3] The whole man involves the person as subject-object, free as well as determined. The whole of reality includes the Almighty. (The atheist by definition has prostituted the nature of responsibility.)

God is not only participant in but central to life. To exclude Him is not simply to restrict the content but to miss the crux of human existence. The presence and nearness of God is the foundation on which the psalm is raised (vs. 1). God is in the here and now, at the fulcrum of life rather than at its periphery.

What is the significance of God's presence? It suggests that we may engage life. Men of faith accept "the present. When the new comes into the present they assess it and respond constructively to it, whether for use or dismissal. They suffer from no fixation but neither are they driven by fugitiveness."[4] Where fear obscures the alternatives and chokes off motivation, the presence of God grants man the permission to act. Man becomes the creative being God intends for one formed in His image. Life makes a demand to which the Christian can respond in the affirmative. Fear says "no," but faith "yes."

Not only does God's presence provide man with an openness to life, but it gives him a purpose for being. Life is a gift to be lived to God's glory. Augustine warns: "Do not invoke, before thou confess; confess, and invoke. For Him whom thou art invoking, unto thyself thou callest."[5] Man calls in vain to a God whose way he will not tolerate, but faith answers the question of life's meaning. It knows why.

To permission and purpose must be added the power to live as

[3]Bonhoeffer, *Ethics*, p. 258.
[4]Ferré, *op. cit.*, p. 17.
[5]Aurelius Augustine, *Expositions on the Book of Psalms*, p. 350.

guaranteed by God's presence. While man is urged to introspection, analysis can lead to paralysis. This is especially true in a situation void of the forgiveness and restoration of God—insight here is crippling. The believer knows a victory which has overcome the world (John 16:33; I John 5:4); his encouragement includes divine enablement.

I–YOU–THOU–IT   *God in the real world 'its'*

God is present in the course of life. He does not have to be searched out in a mystic fashion, but awaits man in the routine of life. As Bonhoeffer suggests: "God encounters us not only as a Thou, but also disguised as an it. . . . Faith demands this elasticity of behavior. Only so can we stand our ground in each situation as it comes along, and turn it to gain."[6] That is, life is situational, but the situation always depends on God's presence. We do not have to feel for Him as if unsure of His promise, but we may accept our responsibility with confidence. Our concern is not with whether He walks with us, but whether we walk with Him.

A pointed break in the tenor of the psalm at verse 2 implies a happening of some consequence. The situation is a threat to the serenity expressed in verse 1 but an opportunity to rely upon the presence of the Almighty (vs. 6).

Christianity is a troubled faith, living as it does in tension with life's departure from the ideal. There are always the injustices, irreverences, and tragedies of human existence. An easy faith would be no faith at all, for it would close its eyes to the real world. However, the absence of faith provides no good alternative, rejecting all meaning because of the problems encountered. The resolution is neither escape nor despair, but facing life with God in confidence.

God speaks. The personal pronoun is emphatic (vs. 2), as if to say that the Almighty is not upset by the threatening situation. The matters of place, time, and means are of divine prerogative. Man is tempted to make Deity follow a prescribed pattern of behavior, a calculated agenda to which He is obligated. The re-

---

[6]Bonhoeffer, *Letters and Papers from Prison*, p. 124.

sult is that one not only accepts this static concept of God but circumscribes himself in the same manner.

The text helps us recapture the dynamic nature of existence (vss. 2-3). As Viktor Frankl reminds us, "Our answer must consist, not in talk and meditation, but in right action and in right conduct. Life ultimately means taking the responsibility to find the right answer to its problems and to fulfill the tasks which it constantly sets for each individual. These tasks, and therefore the meaning of life, differ from man to man, and from moment to moment."[7] Every situation is characterized by its uniqueness, and there is one course of action best for that occasion. Man is responsible to find and act according to his insight.

Ethics, then, is situational, if we mean by this that decisions must at least in part reflect the unique character of the given circumstances. There are no pat answers, no godly gimmicks, no simple directions. Life is complex, and faith faces out on life.

The situation, however, must not be allowed to swallow up the subject. Joseph Fletcher explains his view: "Situation ethics puts people at the center of concern, not things. Obligation is to persons, not to things; to subjects, not objects. The legalist is a *what* asker (What does the law say?); the situationist is a *who* asker (Who is to be helped?)"[8] The situation exists for man, not man for the situation (Mark 2:27).

Fletcher is right in as far as he goes, but he stops critically short. In thinking to be extreme, he has failed to be sufficiently radical. He has reached for the human factor but neglected the divine. God is the center around which life orbits (vs. 1). Ethics is not only situational but humanistic, and not simply humanistic but theistic.

While man may feel God's presence, His nature and acts are difficult to comprehend. The deliverance of Israel left behind the destruction of Egypt. The grand victory of Calvary reduced the disciples to confusion. Even the glorious event of the resurrection proved to be the cause of stumbling to the Greeks. God's acts must be interpreted by His words (vss. 2-3).

---

[7]Frankl, *Man's Search for Meaning*, p. 77.
[8]Joseph Fletcher, *Situation Ethics*, p. 50.

The divine word makes the difference between discovering God as the disguised *It* and not discovering Him at all—the vital contrast between a world in which God is thoroughly engaged and one which has absorbed Him. Man not only finds God in the world but faces life with Him. He is at the same moment searching out and serving the Revealed One.

Living with an articulate Deity is a peculiarly demanding experience. Truth is threatening. It promises to upset the *status quo*, to dissolve certain of those means by which satisfaction has been obtained and to thrust persons into untried situations. Christ, as truth embodied, was the most unsettling Person who ever lived. Men were drawn from their personal aspirations at His call. The crucifixion was the final testimony to the fact that He could not be ignored.

The cross is still a scandal, a threat to man's insulation against God's will, and a call to those concerned with it. There cannot be rest while divine holiness struggles with the world of injustice, and divine mercy with man in need.

God is concerned with the *it*, for Christian living is a concrete exercise. This "is not solely a matter of moral character; it is also a matter of correct appreciation of real situations and of serious reflection upon them."[9] I knew a woman whose conversation was punctuated with references to God's faithfulness, but whose reputation was of doubtful character. While her experience may have had some validity, it failed to demonstrate genuineness to the degree that it remained abstract.

The *it* is not the whole picture—only the condition where divine-human encounter takes place. Satan's alternative is not falsehood but part truth. He torments man with guilt void of grace, with duty lacking direction. Balance is necessary. The Christian (I) can not pronounce the blessing of God (Thou) on the man in need (you), and fail to meet his physical need (it).

Man may entrust himself to the situation when it is understood in its totality. Christ accepted even the cross in the framework of His Father's will. Truth which does not engage life becomes ambiguous, losing its pointedness; it becomes censorious, a weapon

---

[9]Bonhoeffer, *Ethics*, p. 364.

of injury, and/or curious, degenerating into idle discussion. The Christian does not *send* God's word, but *takes* it with him, and finds its application in the situation. He will learn, over and over again, what it means that "all things work together for good for those who love God" (Rom. 8:28), as he lives life without isolation from God, man, or conditions.

Sensitivity to the situation must be cultivated. There are words appropriate to the intimacy of the home, never meant to be shared in public. Who has not been embarrassed by a lack of propriety on the part of others and himself? Bonhoeffer imagines a child being questioned by his teacher and before the members of the class concerning the alleged drunkenness of his father. Such crudeness is repugnant.

This is not to suggest that wrong will go unchallenged, but the time and manner are of crucial importance. Christ knew when to whip the money-changers, but He also comforted the socially ostracized. His disciples must learn His sense of judgment, and this is a product of living in the fullness of every situation.

Life, accordingly, is opportunity. Each moment must be judged on its own merits and liabilities (vss. 2-3). It will be considered in the light of relationship (divine and human) and responsibility (personal and collective). Life draws upon the accumulated wisdom of experience and the revelation of God. His word is revolutionary, recasting life within the perspective of creative possibility.

CONFORMED

The tone of the psalm again shifts with verse 4, and man's presumption comes to the fore (vss. 4-8). Pride is inordinate self-esteem, not self-respect. The distinction is strikingly illustrated in Paul's boast: "But let me not boast, except in the cross of our Lord Jesus Christ" (Gal. 6:14). At first glance, it seems that Paul meant to exclude appreciation of everything except Christ's sacrifice. The context proves differently. He enjoins men to render service worthy of esteem (Gal. 6:4), not limiting their commendation to the benefits of Christian fellowship (6:1-2).

What, then, did Paul mean? The larger context provides an

answer. The epistle to the Galatians reflects the intense struggle with the Judaizers, which had turned the work among the Gentiles into utter confusion. Paul rejects the past advantage supposed by the circumcision, and the partisan spirit the Judaizers fostered. His boasting is rather in the unity in Christ, which breaks down the barrier between Jew and Greek, and maintains the fellowship without distinction. He does not disparage personal or interpersonal worth, but only the inordinate estimation of such.

The nature of the problem will come into better focus as we follow the psalmist's reasoning in verses 4 to 8. Pride is deceptive. It assumes, as in this case, that the resolution of events is quite within human prerogative (vs. 6). A delusion of this magnitude is critical. The man who holds it exists in a dream world, shocked to awareness occasionally as he trips over the hard realities of life. He tries to reorder experience away from God and around himself, while the failure of life to conform to his specification continues to frustrate him.

Pride is also dictatorial (vss. 6-7) "This is its most intolerable pose: for reasons that it does not feel called upon to give, it assumes the prerogatives of the judge and executes its arbitrary pseudo justice solely in terms of the whim that at the moment flatters its posture."[10] Pride readily dons religious garb in order to sanction its demands upon another person. One can hardly imagine a more serious offense than oppressing man in the name of God.

We may imply from the text that pride is dilatory, causing man to delay in accepting his God-given responsibilities. It wastes time in idle boasts, while overlooking the weightier matters of living. Man forgets that life is not for his entertainment, but a demand upon his service. Pride turns the world topsy-turvy, higgledy-piggledy. Man waits for the world to come to him instead of taking the necessary initiative. He errs, not in gratification over a job well done, but in greed for an honor not deserved.

To the characterization of pride as deceptive, dictatorial, and dilatory must be added its destructiveness (vs. 8). The figure of God's cup of wrath is a familiar one, and suggests the impervious

---

[10]Edwin McNeill Poteat, *The Interpreter's Bible*, IV, p. 402.

nature of the moral inebriate and his incapacity caused by violating theonomous law.[11] In the certainty of destruction, the promise of the cup poured out on pride, "we again learn what estimate we ought to form of the providence of God—that we ought to regard it as exercising its control by an ever-present energy over every part of our life."[12]

Only when we undertake to see the grim reality of God's wrath hanging over man can we begin to appreciate grace and forgiveness. Paul Tournier tells of a patient who warned him at her first consultation that she was uninterested in and would not entertain religious matters. Time passed. She was curious as to her inhibitions: "I wonder if it isn't pride which paralyses me like this." Tournier observed: "Everybody is proud . . . I am as proud as you are." The patient was taken back by the admission. "You are not proud." Tournier demurred. She expressed alarm: "What you say is frightful! If everybody is proud whatever he does, then there is no solution." The doctor replied: "Yes, there is a solution, one only, but I cannot tell you of it, as it is a religious one, and you have asked me not to talk to you about religion." The patient now pressed for his answer, and Tournier summarized: "The solution is that I am a proud man who has been forgiven."[13]

Each warning of judgment implies the call to repentance and the promise of forgiveness. The admonition is intended to bring man to his senses, rather than confirm him in his fault. Justice does not preclude but requires grace. The present is man's opportunity for salvation (II Cor. 6:2), since God is present and His promises sure. However, man must respond to God with consideration of his propensity to pride, or he will manipulate even the service of God to his own ends and become the religious hypocrite. Better things than this are expected, the psalmist says.

TRANSFORMED

The remaining verses (vss. 9-10) stand in sharp contrast to man's presumption. The freedom which man asserts to gain his

---

[11]Psalms 11:6, 60:3; Isaiah 51:17; Jeremiah 25:15; Revelation 14:10, 16:19, 18:6.

[12]Calvin, *Commentary on the Book of Psalms*, III, p. 191.

[13]Tournier, *op. cit.*, p. 211.

autonomy proves suicidal, while the servitude of God brings freedom indeed. The distinction holds exciting possibilities.

When Jean Paul Sartre defines man as being-having-freedom-within-the-limits-of-a-situation, he adds: "Authenticity, it is almost needless to say, consists in having a true and lucid consciousness of the situation, in assuming the responsibilities and risks that it involves, in accepting it in pride or humiliation, sometimes in horror and hate."[14] In other words, the present consists of freedom, awareness of the limits set by the situation, and acceptance of the attendant responsibilities. These ideas may be translated into Christian usage.

Freedom is the ability to modify determinants in connection with personal ideals and goals. The Christian's ideals aspire to those of his Lord (Phil. 1:21) and his goals reflect his calling in Christ (Phil. 3:14). He is of all men most free to be himself, to repudiate the carbon copy, and to live the dynamic life of fellowship with the Savior.

There is also a stoic quality to Christianity, a willingness to accept life as one finds it by the grace of God. Yet, this is not meant to suggest complacency. A dynamic optimism allows the Christian faith to sweep beyond stark defiance of conditions: "What is impossible under one set of conditions becomes possible under another; and Christianity undertakes to supply the conditions, to generate the spiritual dynamism required to render its injunctions practicable."[15] Progress seldom comes quickly, and never without cost. One plants, another waters, but there is ever the confidence that God will supply the increase (I Cor. 3:6-7).

The accent in responsibility for the Christian is on response. His life is a relationship. While obedient to God's precepts and faithful to his Lord, the term which best describes his experience is love (agapē). It is the path to true freedom.

Love is attraction. It cannot desist from talking of the Loved One and honoring Him (vs. 9). Yet care must be taken in the way that ardent affection is applied as a test for spirituality: "Some people are 'cold' by temperament; that may be a misfor-

[14]Jean-Paul Sartre, *Anti-Semite and Jew*, p. 90.
[15]Bowman, *op. cit.*, p. 14.

tune for them, but it is no more a sin than having a bad digestion is a sin; and it does not cut them out from the chance, or excuse them from the duty, of learning charity."[16]   Persons differ temperamentally. Neither bursting into ecstasy at the slightest provocation nor keeping a cool head gives one reason to boast over his associates. The expression of love is as diversified as the persons who experience its wonder.

Christian love is action. *Agapē* is seeking love; it does not wait for encouragement nor withdraw in offense. It is sacrificing love, voluntarily offering and faithfully fulfilling the requirement for reconciliation. There is no disparity between promise and performance. If the Church must call attention to its love, it has ceased to love as it should. True love puts works where its words are.

Love is acquisition. It is the efficient means of claiming the present for Christ (I Cor. 13). Paul's elaboration of love comes in the middle of a discussion of spiritual endowments. The Corinthian church prided itself on its gifts, and each member coveted the most ostentatious. Paul sought to correct the situation by pointing out that gifts are provided as God wills for the building up of the Church. He urged the Corinthians to seek the more edifying gifts, though not to the exclusion of others. He then outlined the far better way of love.

Paul pushed his argument, step by step: "Suppose I have the greatest breadth of articulation; without love my words would be empty. Suppose I have comprehension, extending into the hidden things and expanding to the breadth of knowledge, coupled with wonder-working faith and capable of expressing it; without love I am a cipher." Paul appears to be moving from the more to less obvious occasions for unloving *zeal*: "Suppose I were a faithful steward of all I possess, and even surrendered my own body to torture—since my purposes are wrong, without love it helps me not in the least."

The orator may become enamored by his oratory, the student by his knowledge, and the steward by his good deeds. Without love the oratory is meaningless, the knowledge nil, and the deeds unnoted.

---

[16]Lewis, *Mere Christianity*, p. 101.

Paul goes on to describe love (in the words of the Williams' translation):

> Love is so patient and so kind;
> Love never boils with jealousy;
> It never boasts, is never puffed with pride;
> It does not act with rudeness, or insist upon its rights;
> It never gets provoked, it never harbors evil thoughts;
> Is never glad when wrong is done,
> But always glad when truth prevails;
> It bears up under anything,
> It exercises faith in everything,
> It keeps up hope in everything,
> It gives us power to endure in anything.

"Love is this . . . not that, this . . . not that." The pedagogy is elementary, perhaps dramatizing the childishness of the Corinthian believers. Love is patient—persisting through testing and slow in avenging wrong done; kind—cooperating with others. It rejoices with truth—celebrating the triumph of right; it bears up—holding up under all burdens; believes—thinking constructively; hopes—anticipating success; endures—refusing to flee under fire. Conversely, love is not jealous—becoming envious or contentious; does not boast—lauding itself; is not proud—swelling with conceit —or rude—causing others to be embarrassed at the unmannerly behavior; does not seek its own—forgetting others in the cause of self-aggrandizement; does not get provoked—being irritated to anger; does not think evil—dwelling on that which is unwholesome; is not glad over wrong—sympathizing with the wrongdoing of associates.

Paul brings out the specific-universal nature of love: love "bears up under *anything*," "exercises faith in *everything*," "keeps up hope in *everything*," and "gives us power to endure in *anything*." Paul Ramsey observes: "Love for men in general often means merely . . . a selfish sociability, while love for neighbor *for his own sake* insists upon a single-minded orientation of a man's primary intention toward *this* individual neighbor with all his concrete needs."[17] Love requires a clearly defined object. A diffused

---

[17]Paul Ramsey, *Basic Christian Ethics*, p. 95.

sentimentality, on the other hand, may rationalize the lack of love or even excuse itself from having true love.

The individual is himself an object of his love. Erich Fromm points this out: "Not only others, but we ourselves are the *object* of our feelings and attitudes; the attitudes toward others and toward ourselves, far from being contradictory, are basically conjunctive."[18] Selfishness is detrimental to oneself as well as others, while self-love sets the tone for a general respect and understanding.

Love implies totality as well as specificity: "Love always involves persons with each other in the totality of their being; to be concerned with another for less than his whole self is to have something less than true love for him."[19] We may like or dislike certain personality traits, but we either love or hate persons.

Paul continues his description of love:

> Love never fails;
> If there are prophesies, they will be set aside;
> If now exist ecstatic speakings, they will cease;
> If there is knowledge, it will soon be set aside;
>
> . . . .
>
> And so these three, faith, hope, and love endure,
> But the greatest of them is love.
> (I Cor. 13:8, 13, Williams)

His climax is that "love never fails."

Having affirmed that love remains stalwart, Paul returns to the subject of spiritual gifts. The triplet of faith, hope, and love surpass spiritual gifts because of their *durability*. "Out of these" love is greatest. Charles Hodge interprets the superiority: "Throughout that chapter the ground of preference of one gift to others is made to consist in its superior usefulness. This is Paul's standard: and judged by this rule, love is greater than either faith or hope. Faith saves ourselves, but love benefits others."[20]

_____

[18]Erich Fromm, *Man for Himself*, p. 129.
[19]Arthur Vogel, *The Christian Person*, p. 83.
[20]Charles Hodge, *An Exposition of the First Epistle to the Corinthians*, p. 276.

Love resists our most arduous efforts to capture it in verbal symbols. Lacking love, Sartre vividly describes other people as hell—a restriction of life. With love we find liberation of spirit. It is this contrast that the psalmist draws in the concluding verse of his psalm as he describes the legacies of the wicked and the righteous (vs. 10).

CONCLUSION

"Our enduring task in philosophical endeavor is to become authentic men."[21] Man's concern is not with theoretical knowledge, unless the experience of living hinges upon it, but with living, and life is a condition of the present.

Christ invests the present with meaning and opportunity. While the slave of sin perishes, the servant of Christ abides (John 8:35-36). The contrast between the sinner (vss. 4-8) and the exultation of the believing (vss. 9-10) are similarly observed by the psalmist.

Every moment is qualified by the situation, the self, and the Savior. The Christian can accept himself because God has received him, his lot because God has called him to it, and his future because it is in the keeping of the Almighty. His responsibility makes him painfully sensitive to the situation, but his relationship keeps him joyfully aware of God's presence. The present has continuity with the past, purpose for the future, and meaning for eternity. So the Scripture reads: "Today if you will hear His voice, harden not your heart" (Psa. 95:7b, 8a).

---

[21]Karl Jaspers, *The Perennial Scope of Philosophy*, p. 159.

Bibliography

Allport, Gordon W. "The Open System in Personality Theory," *Theories of Personality*, Lindzey and Hall, eds., 231-239.

Aquinas, Thomas. *Summa Theologica*. Three Volumes. New York: Benzeger Brothers, 1948.

Augustine, Aurelius. *The City of God*. Two Volumes. New York: Hafner Publishing Company, 1948.

———. *Enchiridion*. In *Nicene and Post-Nicene Fathers*, Schaff, ed., III, 237-276.

———. *Expositions on the Book of Psalms*. Vol. VIII of *Nicene and Post-Nicene Fathers*, Schaff, ed.

The Babylonian Talmud. Thirty-five Volumes. London: The Soncino Press, 1952.

Barclay, Oliver R. *Guidance: Some Biblical Principles*. Third Edition. London: Inter-Varsity Fellowship, 1962. Chicago: Inter-Varsity Press.

Bonhoeffer, Dietrich. *The Communion of Saints*. New York: Harper & Row, 1960.

———. *The Cost of Discipleship*. New York: The Macmillan Company, 1963. Copyright 1948 by the Macmillan Company.

———. *Ethics*. New York: The Macmillan Company, 1963. Copyright © 1955 by The Macmillan Company.

———. *Letters and Papers from Prison*. New York: The Macmillan Company, 1962. Copyright 1953 by The Macmillan Company.

Bowman, Archibald A. *The Absurdity of Christianity and Other Essays*. New York: The Liberal Arts Press, 1958.

Brandon, Owen. *The Battle for the Soul*. Philadelphia: The Westminster Press, 1959. London: Hodder and Stoughton Limited.

Bultmann, Rudolph. *History and Eschtology*. New York: Harper & Row, 1957.

Calvin, John. *Commentary on the Book of Psalms*. Five Volumes. Grand Rapids: William B. Eerdmans, 1949.

———. *Institutes of the Christian Religion*. Two Volumes. Philadelphia: Presbyterian Board of Christian Education, 1936.

Coe, George A. *The Psychology of Religion*. Chicago: University of Chicago Press, 1916.

Cohen, Abraham. *The Psalms*. London: The Soncino Press, 1962.

Collingwood, Robin G. *The Idea of History.* Oxford: Clarendon Press, 1946.

Cox, David. *Jung and St. Paul.* London: Longmans, Green and Company, 1956. New York: Association Press, 1959.

Cox, Harvey. *The Secular City.* New York: The Macmillan Company, 1965.

Cyprian. *The Treatises.* In *Ante-Nicene Fathers,* Roberts and Donaldson, eds., V, 421-557.

Delitzsch, Franz. *Biblical Commentary on the Psalms.* Three Volumes. Edinburgh: T. & T. Clark, 1871.

Dodds, Marcus. *The Epistle of the Hebrews.* Volume IV of *Expositor's Greek Testament,* W. Robertson Nicoll, ed. Grand Rapids: Wm. B. Eerdmans, 1952.

Dresser, Horatio. *Outlines of the Psychology of Religion.* New York: Thomas Y. Crowell, 1929.

Eliot, T. S. *Collected Poems 1909-1962.* New York: Harcourt, Brace and World, 1964. London: Faber & Faber, Ltd.

Epistle of Barnabas. In *Ante-Nicene Fathers,* Roberts and Donaldson, eds., I, 137-149.

Ferré, Nels F. S. *The Finality of Faith.* New York: Harper & Row, Inc., 1963.

Fisher, Fred L. *Prayer in the New Testament.* Philadelphia: The Westminster Press, 1964.

Fletcher, Joseph. *Situation Ethics.* Philadelphia: The Westminster Press, 1966.

Frankl, Viktor E. *Man's Search for Meaning.* Boston: Beacon Press, 1963.

_____. *The Doctor and the Soul.* New York: Alfred A. Knopf, 1955.

Freud, Sigmund. *New Introductory Lectures on Psychoanalysis.* New York: W. W. Norton, 1933.

Fromm, Erich. "Character and the Social Process," In *Theories of Personality.* Lindzey and Hall, eds.

_____. *Man for Himself.* New York: Holt, Rinehart and Winston, 1947.

_____. *Psychoanalysis and Religion.* New Haven: Yale University Press, 1950.

Gladden, Washington. *Social Salvation.* New York: Houghton, Mifflin and Company, 1902.

Gordon, Cyrus H. *The World of the Old Testament.* Garden City: Doubleday & Company, 1958.

Greenwell, Dora and P. T. Forsyth. *The Power of Prayer*. London: Hodder and Stoughton, n.d.

Hartt, Julian N. *The Lost Image of Man*. Baton Rouge: Louisiana State University Press, 1963.

Hastings, James, editor. *The Doctrine of Prayer*. New York: Charles Scribner's Sons, 1915.

Herberg, Will. "Biblical Faith as Heilsgeschichte," *The Christian Scholar*, XXXIX (March, 1956), 25-31.

Hertzberg, Arthur, editor. *Judaism*. New York: George Braziler, 1961. (Washington Square Press, 1963).

——. *The Zionist Idea*. Garden City: Doubleday & Company, 1959.

Hodge, Charles. *An Exposition of the First Epistle of the Corinthians*. London: Hodder & Stoughton, 1857. (Grand Rapids: Wm. B. Eerdmans, 1950, reprint edition.)

Homer. *The Iliad*. Translated by Richmond Lattimore. Chicago: University of Chicago Press, 1951.

Howe, Reuel L. *The Miracle of Dialogue*. New York: Seabury Press, 1963.

The Interpreter's Bible. Twelve Volumes. G. A. Buttrick, ed. New York: Abingdon Press, 1951-1963.

Jaspers, Karl. *Man in the Modern Age*. Garden City: Doubleday & Company, 1957.

——. *Origin and Goal of History*. Translated by Michael Bullock. New Haven: Yale University Press, 1953.

——. *The Perennial Scope of Philosophy*. Translated by R. Manheim. New York: Philosophical Library, 1949.

Jeremias, Joachim. *The Problem of the Historical Jesus*. Philadelphia: Fortress Press, 1964.

Josephus, Flavius. *Antiquities of the Jews*. In *The Works of Flavius Josephus*. Philadelphia: International Press, n.d.

Jung, Carl. "Patterns of Behavior and Archetypes," In *Theories of Personality*, Lindzey and Hall, eds., 59-76.

Kant, Immanuel. *Lectures on Ethics*. New York: Harper & Row, 1963.

Kaufmann, Walter, editor. *Existentialism from Dostoevsky to Sartre*. Cleveland: The World Publishing Company, 1956.

Keyser, Leander. *A Handbook of Christian Psychology*. Burlington: The Lutheran Literary Board, 1928.

King, Winston L. *Buddhism and Christianity: Some Bridges of Understanding*. Philadelphia: The Westminster Press, 1962.

Knight, George A. F., editor. *Jews and Christians: Preparation for Dialogue*. Philadelphia: The Westminster Press, 1965.

Lee, Robert and Martin Marty, editors. *Religion and Social Conflict*. New York: Oxford University Press, 1964.

Lewis, C. S. *Mere Christianity*. New York: The Macmillan Company, 1952. Copyright 1943, 1945, 1952 by the Macmillan Company.

_____. *The Problem of Pain*. New York: The Macmillan Company, 1962 (paperback).

_____. *The Screwtape Letters*. New York: The Macmillan Company, 1943.

Ligon, Ernest. *The Psychology of the Christian Personality*. New York: The Macmillan Company, 1961.

The Life of Trust: Being a Narrative of the Lord's Dealings with George Muller. New York: Crowell Publishing Company, n.d.

Lindzey, Gardner and Calvin Hall, editors. *Theories of Personality: Primary Sources and Research*. New York: John Wiley and Sons, 1965.

Locke, John. *The Reasonableness of Christianity*. Boston: T. B. Wait and Company, 1811.

Luchins, Abraham and Edith. *Rigidity of Behavior*. Eugene: University of Oregon Books, 1959.

Luther, Martin. *Open Letter Concerning the Hard Book Against the Peasants*. In *Works of Martin Luther*. Philadelphia: A. J. Holman, IV, 157-184.

Marcel, Gabriel. *Homo Viator*. New York: Harper & Row, 1965.

Maslow, Abraham H. "Some Basic Propositions of a Growth and Self-Actualization Psychology." In *Theories of Personality*, Lindzey & Hall, eds.

McCoy, Charles. "The Churches and Protest Movements for Racial Justice." In *Religion and Social Conflict*, Lee and Marty, eds., 37,54.

McKenzie, John G. *Guilt, Its Meaning and Significance*. New York: Abingdon Press, 1963.

Milton, John. *Paradise Lost*.

Mouroux, John. *The Meaning of Man*. Translated by W. H. Blake. Garden City: Doubleday & Company, 1948.

Murray, James. *An Introduction to Christian Psycho-Therapy*. New York: Charles Scribner's Sons, 1938.

Niebuhr, H. Richard. *Christ and Culture*. New York: Harper & Row, 1956.

Niebuhr, Reinhold. *The Nature and Destiny of Man*. New York: Charles Scribner's Sons, 1941.

Norborg, Svene. *Varieties of Christian Experience*. Minneapolis: Augsburg Publishing House, 1937.

Okey, Thomas, editor. *The Little Flowers of St. Francis*, et. al. New York: E. P. Dutton, 1908.

Oman, John. *Grace and Personality*. New York: Association Press, 1961.

Origen. *Contra Celsum*. In *Ante-Nicene Fathers*, Roberts and Donaldson, eds., IV, 573-669.

Petry, Ray C. *Christian Eschatology and Social Thought*. New York: Abingdon Press, 1956.

Phillips, J. B. *Plain Christianity*. New York: The Macmillan Company, 1954.

Ramsey, Paul. *Basic Christian Ethics*. New York: The Macmillan Company, 1954.

Roberts, Alexander and James Donaldson, editors. *Ante-Nicene Fathers*. Nine Volumes. Grand Rapids: William B. Eerdmans, 1951.

Robertson, E. H. *Man's Estimate of Man*. Naperville, Ill.: SCM Book Club, 1958.

Robinson, H. Wheeler. *The Christian Doctrine of Man*. Edinburgh: T. & T. Clark, 1947.

Sartre, Jean-Paul. *Anti-Semite and Jew*. New York: Schocken Books, 1948.

———. "Existentialism is a Humanism." In *Existentialism from Dostoevsky to Sartre*, Kaufmann, ed., 187-311.

Schaff, Phillip, editor. *Nicene and Post-Nicene Fathers*. Fourteen Volumes. New York: Christian Literature, 1900. (Grand Rapids: Wm. B. Eerdmans, 1952-1956.)

Schall, James. "The Social Mission of Christianity." In *Curent Trends in Theology*, Wolf and Schall, eds., 287-311.

Schweitzer, Albert. *The Quest for the Historical Jesus*. London: A. & C. Black, 1936.

Shedd, Russell P. *Man in Community*. Grand Rapids: William B. Eerdmans, 1964.

Smith, Page. *The Historian and History*. New York: Alfred A. Knopf, 1964.

Spurgeon, Charles H. *The Treasury of David*. Seven Volumes.

London: Marshall Brothers, 1870. (Three Volumes; Grand Rapids: Zondervan Publishing House, 1964.)

Stacy, W. David. *The Pauline View of Man*. New York: The Macmillan Company, 1956.

Stauffer, Ethelbert. *Jesus and His Story*. New York: Alfred A. Knopf, 1960.

Stott, John R. W. *Basic Christianity*. Grand Rapids: William B. Eerdmans, 1957.

Strasser, Stephan. *Phenomenology and the Human Sciences*. Pittsburg: Duquesne University Press, 1963.

Tacitus. *Annales*. Volume I of *The Works of Cornelius Tacitus*. New York: Harper and Brothers, 1858.

Tertullian. *Apologeticum*. In *Ante-Nicene Fathers*, Roberts and Donaldson, eds., III, 17-55.

_____. *The Chaplit*. In *Ante-Nicene Fathers*, III. 93-103.

_____. *The Shows*. In *Ante-Nicene Fathers*, III. 79-91.

Tillich, Paul. *Systematic Theology*. Three Volumes. Chicago: University of Chicago Press, 1951-1963.

_____. *The Eternal Now*. New York: Charles Scribner's Sons, 1963.

Tournier, Paul. *Guilt and Grace*. New York: Harper & Row, 1962.

Toynbee, Arnold. *Civilization on Trial* and *The World and the West*. Cleveland: World Publishing Company, 1962.

Trueblood, David Elton. *Philosophy of Religion*. New York: Harper & Row, 1957.

Trumbull, H. Clay. *Studies in Oriental Social Life*. Philadelphia: J. D. Wattles and Company, 1894.

Ungersma, Aaron J. *The Search for Meaning*. Philadelphia: The Westminster Press, 1961.

Vogel, Arthur A. *The Christian Person*. New York: Seabury Press, 1963.

Williams, Charles B. *The New Testament in the Language of the People*. Chicago: Moody Press, 1953.

White, Ernest. *Christian Life and the Unconscious*. New York: Harper & Row, 1955.

Wise, Carroll. *Mental Health and the Bible*. New York: Harper & Row, 1956.

Wolf, Donald and James Schall, editors. *Current Trends in Theology*. Garden City: Doubleday & Company, 1965.

Woodworth, Robert S. and M. R. Sheehan. *Contemporary*

Schools of Psychology. Third Edition. New York: Ronald Press, 1964.

Zorn, Raymond O. *Church and Kingdom.* Philadelphia: Presbyterian and Reformed Publishing Company, 1962.

3 8 " Thesis is not explicit in anything,
          but is implicit ... everywhere"   (on proof ? fulness
                                                sense ?)

187 "Satan torments man w/ guilt void of grace"

14 ✓ Frankl : "... actually we ought not interrogate God...   45 ganglion
      rather he'... life without answers : ah is what   facticity 159
      we're doing w/ et of 9 of life ..."
              (on responsibility)

196 Tourneir, "Everyone is freed .. when their belief is genuine"
          ~T4p

                                      Suervier   1698 ?
                                                          Hope

61 II Ad 1 " godliness is not same as being good"
169 II Frankl, II Ad 3- apos. to serious people must have a futa
170   believe in T
175 II P. 3:11 X

168 Seen .. bell.

                                                P4 T4 4 rabbis at the town's
                                                   door - only 1 laughed,
         there no   for he saw to the end 4   B
         hau   no continuing... city must be why ? pros 144 11-12
This is a good way to select PS's
In a sense. And such, even pres bldg-   33 I Jn - sin to doubt is
      to make e und PS, contemprary.   usual sin, but "turn of th
        (a quick keep do to preaches)   x   backs", apostasy.
PS 8   34 #5 Gen 3 - "godliness"
                                              35 Gen 4 X
  (14) 15.20 P 120
   32   75 Rom 12:1-2 (From)
   1-2
   23   193 I Co 13 - (William
   22   trans)
   87
   20   (13) Josh 24:15
   52
   135   22 Ezek 18:4-5 -
    67   as Adam kland enosh
    75   in God's day, in tree -
                                          Israel kland letter parents